VOICES FROM THE CROWD

Against the H-Bomb

VOICES FROM THE CROWD

Against the H-Bomb

edited by David Boulton

DUFOUR EDITIONS • PHILADELPHIA

Printed in Great Britain for Dufour Editions, Philadelphia
Library of Congress Catalog Card Number 65-25493

CONTENTS

CONTENTS *continued*

FOREWORD

It may be instructive to consider for a moment what would have happened over these past six or seven years or what would be the situation now if there had been no Campaign for Nuclear Disarmament, no CND, in existence at all.

Aldermaston would denote nothing much more than a disfigured Berkshire village. The road via Reading, Maidenhead and Slough to Turnham Green would not be stamped on the minds of some thirty or forty thousand citizens of this country with its full indelible ugliness. The decadence of modern youth could not be attributed to its distaste for committing mass murder or, rather, its insistence on stressing the point so shamelessly to its elders. The Sandys Defence White Papers of 1957 and 1958 might still be considered masterly essays in strategic doctrine. Who knows – Mr. Sandys might still be the Minister of Defence instead of the last but four, or is it six? Massive retaliation might still be regarded as a respectable idea. That, in case you've forgotten, is what we pledged ourselves to do to the Russians in certain circumstances and it would be wrong to make any accusation of betrayal; the pledge has never been withdrawn.

But to continue. Without CND, would the Labour Party have atrophied? Scarborough would have remained just another seaside resort. Life for Labour leaders would have been almost cushy. Detective-Sergeant Challenor would still have been accepted as a credit to the Force. And what you may well ask, would Constantine FitzGibbon, Robert Conquest and the rest have had to write about? Suppose the kissing had never started! Whatever could the Communists have been up to if there was nowhere to infiltrate? The awkward, hypothetical questions are endless.

Yet even without the answers it is possible to make one modest, indisputable assertion. Without CND, the world-wide debate about the most perilous invention in history would have been less noisy, less extensive, less widespread across so many frontiers. It might, so opponents could argue, have been more clear-headed, more well-conceived, less acrimonious, less hysterical. Even if these unwarrantable claims are conceded the other test remains. Is this a debate in which everyone should join or is it one to be left to the experts, the scientists who know, the military advisers, the very few? The differing responses to that question go to the root of our democracy and our political system. This was appreciated by many who joined CND and was another reason for its appeal.

It may be that the statesmen would have worked to secure a test ban treaty with no less earnestness if there had been none of the pressure which CND helped to exert. It may be that for the six years prior to the signing of the treaty all the signatories who subsequently rejoiced at the banishment of the radiation and other horrors involved in testing were as secretly alarmed as CNDers and were merely suppressing or distorting the facts out of an excessive and misplaced consideration for the tender feelings of the public. (Here, by the way, I am prompted to suggest that there should be a companion volume to go with this one – an anthology of nuclear lies. One of the most staggering and scandalous facts of the nuclear age has been the arrogance with which the leading statesmen of the world have tried to keep within tiny cliques the truth about a matter of such supreme consequence to everybody.)

But again one simple assertion cannot be contested. The anti-CNDers, however sweeping or brash their protests, cannot deny that CND forcefully introduced into the debate an element which almost everybody else wanted to keep out. Others thought the argument was principally about politics or strategy. CND insisted that, whatever else the question also was, it was a *moral* one. And who will dare say that this emphasis is wrong? How debasing and dishonourable to the human species it would have been if the question of massive extermination on a scale far exceeding anything known even in Hitler's death camps had been permitted to continue being discussed without the issue of moral responsibility arising. But that is what so many people wanted and still want. CND was never guilty on that charge.

And this brings us to the most explosive point involved, CND's distinctive contribution, the demand for unilateral action by Britain. As it happened, at the first meeting when the organisation was formed in February 1958, it was by no means certain that this clause would be included in CND's programme. Some of those present at the meeting argued that the case for general nuclear disarmament should be presented in more widely-embracing terms. No doubt a few worthwhile public meetings could have been conducted in this style. The Archbishop of Canterbury would doubtless have bestowed his blessing from the outset and might even have marched to and from Aldermaston in such a respectable cause – if there had been any marches. No one can deny the plain fact. CND developed differently from the campaigns that had gone before, provoked furious enthusiams and emnities, and made a spectacular appeal particularly to the young, precisely because it did not take refuge in vague generalities, precisely because it did urge that something could be *done,* precisely because it did pin responsibility on our country, on us.

This is not the place to press the case. Indeed, that is one purpose of this anthology – to show what the standard, temper and tone of the argument was. But, whatever the verdict CND has already one achievement to its credit of which many of us are extremely proud. It made our country the most active and vocal in the world in attempting to arouse mankind to an awareness of the nuclear horror. Without CND, the complacency of those in power would have been even more perilous and contemptible than it was. But, of course, this is only a first, minor victory. The armour-plated smugness of our rulers is only dented. At the moment of writing the most widely-accepted bromide of our statesmen (disseminated by the same people who pretend to favour general disarmament and still put forward plans allegedly designed to serve this end at Geneva) is that the balance of terror keeps the peace and can always be relied – to do so. Nuclear weapons, it seems, have conferred on suffering humanity the matchless boon of perpetual peace. No one advances this inanity with greater assurance than Sir Alec Douglas Home. Which is just another reason why if there was no CND in existence now, it would be necessary to invent it.

MICHAEL FOOT

August 1964

INTRODUCTION

The age of nuclear weapons and potential nuclear warfare is one year short of its twentieth birthday as this anthology is being prepared. Yet nothing here is more than seven years old. Why those twelve silent years, from 1945 to 1957?

One answer would require a history of Britain's militant campaigns for nuclear disarmament, and already of the writing of such histories and purported histories there is no end – and more are promised. Another answer is that these were not silent years at all. Voices of protest, warning and entreaty *were* heard from the crowd, but they were lost in the wind or for one reason or another failed to find a wave-length that would carry them.

But a great many things did begin to happen a dozen years after Hiroshima and Nagasaki numbed men's minds and accustomed them to the idea of genocide. Mothers (and fathers too) who were prepared to live under the shadow of the H-bomb if their betters decreed it to be a regrettable necessity began to understand that this protective weapon, even in peace time, threatened their health and their children's health by its testing. They began to worry, quietly, alone. Then they worried publicly and together.

Within the space of a few months the Suez invasion and the crushing of the Hungarian socialist revolution each shattered the comparative quiet of the long decade of post-war politics. Suez brought thousands onto the streets to register political protest – many of them for the first time in their lives. And Hungary showed how closely the violent power-politics of the old Imperial West were mirrored by the violent power-politics of the new Imperial East.

The atom bomb had become the hydrogen bomb. Now these weapons were carried in regular patrol over the skies of England. Men said that one day, before long, bombers would be obsolete and nuclear weapons would be carried to any part of the globe by rocket. Even in 1957, when the name Polaris had meaning only for the astronomers, there were whispers of a nuclear-tipped missile that would be launched from the impregnability of a roaming submarine and be directed to any city in the world.

So the revolt began. It was a revolt which found no expression in conventional politics. Hopes that it might do so were shattered when Aneurin Bevan steered the 1957 British Labour Party Conference away from its tentative concern with what he contemptuously dismissed as an 'emotional spasm'. With nowhere else to sound, the voices from the crowd, voices against the H-bomb, sounded out from the wilderness. Before long there were so many voices that it was a wilderness no longer.

Protest was not confined to Britain. In the United States a National Committee for a Sane Nuclear Policy actually pre-dated Britain's own CND by a few months, and the CND symbol – a combination of the semaphore signals for N (nuclear) and D (disarmament) – swept across the world. CND movements came into being in almost every major West European country (notably West Germany, Greece, Norway, Sweden, Denmark and France), and in Canada, Australia and New Zealand.

But the British movement remained the focus of the New Dissent, and many of Britain's best-known writers and thinkers were among its spokesmen. This anthology is an attempt to put their voices on record. The selection is inevitably arbitrary. Some who protested most loudly and most persuasively are not represented here, perhaps because they themselves have decided that temporary cries in the darkness are unsuited to the permanency of hard covers, or perhaps (and more often) because their writings always tended to be so deeply embedded in a context of events or argument that transplantation was impossible. (Michael Foot's 'Tribune' articles and speeches are the most prominent of these).

The pieces have been so placed that there should be some benefit from consecutive reading instead of random dipping. I have not followed chronology accurately, though the sweep of the collection does so generally. Again, I have not imposed any formal divisions, though natural groupings – personal testimonies, civil defence, the peace movement's search for new politics – will quickly be apparent.

If this collection should seem to flow more from the heart than the head it should be remembered that it has been no part of my purpose to offer anything like proportional representation as between straight evangelism and the dialectics of peace politics. Most of the voices here are straight from the throat, and they represent a period that is already passing. They registered protest, and in the late 'fifties and early 'sixties that was enough. Now it remains for the Campaign for Nuclear Disarmament to find effective political expression for its protest, and if it cannot *find* it, to go out and *make* it. But that will demand more and different voices, and one day, perhaps, a rather different anthology.

I am indebted to the authors and their original editors, where appropriate, for permission to reproduce their work. Most of them have indicated their intention of donating their share of royalties to the Campaign for Nuclear Disarmament.

April 1964 DAVID BOULTON

Albert Schweitzer

PEACE OR ATOMIC WAR

'Peace or Atomic War?' *was the corporate title of three broadcast talks given from Oslo by Dr Albert Schweitzer on April 28, 29 and 30, 1958. The following text, from the transcript, amalgamates extracts from them.*

Today we have to envisage the menacing possibility of an outbreak of atomic war between Soviet Russia and America. It can only be avoided if the two powers decide to renounce atomic arms.

How has this situation arisen?

In 1945 America succeeded in producing an atom bomb with uranium 235. On August 6, 1945, this bomb was released on Hiroshima and on August 9, on Nagasaki.

America's possession of such a bomb gave her a military advantage over other countries.

In July, 1949 the Soviet Union also possessed such a bomb. And its power was equal to the one which was brought into being by America between 1946 and 1949. Consequently peace between the two powers was maintained on the basis of mutual respect for the bomb of the other.

On October 3, 1952, England exploded its first atom bomb on the Isle of Montebello, on the north-west coast of Australia.

Then to secure an advantage, America took the decision to invite Edward Teller to produce the hydrogen bomb. It was expected that this H-bomb would exceed many times the power of the uranium bomb. This bomb was first released in May, 1951 at Eniwetok on the Pacific atoll Elugelab in October, 1952. On March 1, 1954, at Bikini, one of the group in the Marshall Islands in the Pacific Ocean, the perfected H-bomb was exploded. It was found that the actual power of the explosion was much stronger than was originally expected on the basis of calculations.

But at the same time as America, the Soviet Union also started producing H-bombs, the first of which was exploded on August 12, 1953. Both powers progressed contemporaneously. America invented the atom bomb during the second world war, and subsequently worked on the principles of the rockets which served Germany in those days.

War no longer depends on the ability of mighty aeroplanes to carry bombs to their targets. Now there are guided rockets that can be launched from their starting point and directed with accuracy to a distant target. Missiles are carried by such rockets propelled by a fuel which is constantly being developed in efficiency. The missile carried by the rocket can be an ordinary missile or one which contains a uranium warhead or an H-bomb warhead.

It is said that the Soviet Union certainly disposes of rockets with a range of up to 625 miles, and probably with a range up to 1,100 miles.

America is said to possess rockets with a range of 1,500 miles.

Whether the so-called intercontinental missile with a range of 5,000 miles exists cannot be ascertained. It is assumed that the problem of its production is on the way to being solved, and that both East and West are occupied with its production.

Although an intercontinental rocket is not yet known to be completed, America has to be prepared for submarines shooting such a projectile far into the country. These rockets proceed with immense velocity. It is expected that an intercontinental rocket would not take more than half an hour to cross the oceans with loads of bombs from one to five tons.

How would an atomic war be conducted today? At first the so-called local war – but today there is little difference between a local war and a global war. Rocket missiles will be used up to a range of 1,500 miles. The destruction should not be underestimated, even if caused only by a type of Hiroshima bomb, not to speak of an H-bomb.

It can hardly be expected that an enemy will renounce the use of atom bombs, or the most perfected H-bombs on large cities from the very outset. The H-bomb has a thousandfold stronger development of power than the atom bomb.

It is therefore quite possible that in a future atomic war both rocket projectiles and large bombers will be used together. Rocket projectiles will not replace bombers, but will rather complement them.

The immediate effect of an H-bomb will have a range of several miles. The heat will be 100 million degrees. One can imagine how great the number of city-dwelling human beings who would be destroyed by the pressure of the explosion by flying fragments of glass, by heat and fire and by radio-active waves, even if the attack is only of short duration. The deadly radio-active infection, as a consequence of the explosion would have a range of some 45,000 square miles.

An American general said to some Congressmen:

'If at intervals of 10 minutes 110 H-bombs are dropped over the U.S.A. there would be a casualty list of about 70 million people, besides some thousands of square miles made useless for a whole generation. Those countries like England, West Germany and France could be finished off with 15 to 20 H-bombs.'

President Eisenhower has pointed out, after watching manoeuvres under atomic attack, that defence measures in a future atomic war become useless. In these circumstances all one can do is to pray.

Indeed, not much more can be done in view of an attack by H-bombs than to advise all people living to hide behind very strong walls of stone or cement, and throw themselves on the ground and to cover the back of their heads, and the body if possible, with cloth. In this way it may be possible to escape annihilation and death through radiation. It is essential that those surviving be given food and drink which are not radio-active and that they be transported away from the radio-active district.

It is impossible to erect walls of such thickness for the whole population of a city. Where would the material and the means come from? How would a population have time even to run to safety in such bunkers?

In an atomic war there would be neither conqueror nor vanquished. During such a bombardment both sides would suffer the same fate. A continuous destruction would take place and no armistice or peace proposals could bring it to an end.

When people deal with atomic weapons, no one can say to the other, 'Now the arms must decide'; but only, 'Now we want to commit suicide together, destroying each other mutually....'

There is good reason for an English M.P. saying:

'He who uses atomic weapons becomes subject to the fate of a bee, namely, when it stings it will perish inevitably, for having made use of its sting.'

He who uses atomic weapons to defend freedom would become subject to a similar fate.

Those who conduct an atomic war for such freedom will die, or end their lives miserably. Instead of freedom they will find destruction. Radio-active clouds resulting from a war between East and West would imperil humanity everywhere. There would be no need to use up the remaining stock of atom and H-bombs. There are about 5,000 of them.

An atomic war is therefore the most senseless and lunatic act that could ever take place. At all costs it must be prevented.

Unfortunately a cold war may turn into an atomic war. This danger is made greater today than it has ever been, because of the possibility of employing long-distance rockets.

In days gone by America held to the principle of being, apart from the Soviet Union, the sole owner of atomic weapons. There was no virtue in equipping other countries with atom and H-bombs, for they would not have known what to do with them. But, with the arrival of rocket projectiles of a smaller type and a longer range, the situation is changing. The use of such smaller weapons is possible for lesser countries who are in alliance with the U.S.A. Thus America has deviated from her principle not to put atomic weapons into the hands of other countries, a decision with grave consequences.

On the other hand it is understandable that the U.S.A. wishes to supply the NATO countries with such new weapons for defence against the Soviet Union. The presence of such arms constitutes a new threat to the Soviet Union, opening the way for an atomic war between America and the Soviet Union on European soil. This situation did not exist before. Now the Soviet Union is within range of such rockets from European soil, even as far as Moscow and Kharkov, up to 1,500 miles away.

Rockets of average range could be used for defence purposes by Turkey and Iran against the Soviet Union, into which they could penetrate deeply with such arms accepted from America, and the Soviet Union in turn may now be forced into a situation when it has to defend itself.

Both the U.S.A. and the Soviet Union may now seek alliances with the Middle East by offering such countries financial support. Such quarrels as may occur could start in secret, and unknown events in the Middle East could endanger the peace of the world.

The risk of an atomic war is being increased by the fact that no warning would be given in starting such a war, which could originate in some mere incident. The side that attacks first would have the initial advantage over the attacked, who would at once sustain losses that would reduce his fighting capacity considerably.

The necessity for a round-the-clock alert against attack carries with it the extreme danger of an error in interpreting what appears on a radar screen, when immediate action is imperative, resulting in the outbreak of an atomic war.

Attention was drawn to this danger by the American General Curtis Le May when recently the world was on the brink of such a situation. The radar stations of the American Air Force and American Coastal Command reported that an invasion of unidentified bombers was on the way. Upon this warning the General in command of the strategic bomber force decided to order a reprisal bombardment to commence. However, realising the enormity of his responsibility, he then hesitated. Shortly afterwards it was discovered that the radar stations had made a technical error. What could have happened if a less balanced General had been in his place?

In the future such dangers are likely to increase owing to the fact that small rockets exist which pass through the air with terrific speed, and are difficult to identify, so that defence possibilities become very limited. The defence has only seconds in which to identify the approaching rockets and to counter-attack by exploding these before they can reach their targets, at the same time dispatching bombers to destroy the ramps from which they are launched.

Such decisions cannot be left to the human brain for it works too slowly. They have to be entrusted to an electronic brain. If it appears that enemy rockets are really on the way on the radar screen, calculations as to their distance have to be made to the fraction of a second, so that an immediate start can be made by releasing defence rockets.

All this proceeds automatically. Such is our achievement that we now depend entirely on an electronic brain, and on errors and omissions from which such an instrument cannot be exempt. The making of a decision by means of an electronic brain, though quicker, is not as reliable as the making of a decision by the human brain. At some point the complex mechanism of the electronic brain may become faulty.

These developments lead inevitably to a worsening of the situation. We have to reckon with the fact that the U.S.A. may proceed with the supply of atomic weapons to other countries, trusting them not to use them selfishly or incautiously. Both the other atomic powers are at liberty to do likewise.

Yet, who can guarantee that among the favoured countries in possession of such weapons there may not be black sheep acting on their own, without regard for the consequences? Who is to prevent them? Who is able to make them renounce the use of atomic weapons, even if other countries have decided to make such a decision in common? The dam is breached and it may collapse.

That such anxieties have become very real is shown by a statement on January 13, 1958 on behalf of 9,235 scientists of UNO regarding the cessation of atomic tests. One of their points is the following:

'As long as atomic weapons remain in the hands of the three great powers, an agreement as to their control is possible. However, if the tests continue and extend to other countries in possession of atomic weapons, the risks and responsibilities in regard to an outbreak of an atomic war become all the greater. From every point of view the danger in a future atomic war becomes all the more intense so that an urgent renunciation of atomic weapons becomes absolutely imperative.'

America's attitude to the renunciation of atomic weapons is remarkable. It cannot be otherwise – her conviction is that they should be outlawed, yet at the same time in case this does not come about she strives, with other countries in NATO, to put herself in the most favourable military situation.

Thus America insists that the rockets which she offers to other countries should be accepted as soon as possible. She seeks to hold such a position as enables her to maintain peace by terrifying her opponent. But she is finding that most of the NATO countries are reluctant to acquire the weapons which they are being offered, because of an increasing strengthening of adverse public opinion.

It would be of immense importance if America in this hour of destiny could decide in favour of renouncing atomic weapons, to remove the possibility of an eventual outbreak of an atomic war. The theory of peace through terrifying an opponent by a greater armament can now only heighten the danger of war.

A ray of light in darkness – in December 1957 the Polish Foreign Minister Rapacki made a proposition that Czechoslovakia, East and West Germany should consist of an atom-free zone. If this proposal is accepted and the atom-free zones could be enlarged to include adjoining countries the maintenance of peace would be assured. The beginning of the end of the spectre that overshadows the Soviet Union would become an accomplished fact.

With this sensible proposition, public opinion in Europe is in absolute agreement. It has become convinced, during recent months, that under no circumstances is Europe to become a battlefield for an atomic war between the Soviet Union and America. From this conviction it will no longer deviate. The time is past when a European country could plan secretly to establish itself as a great power by manufacturing atomic weapons exclusively for its own use. Since public opinion would never agree to such an undertaking, it becomes senseless even to prepare secretly for the realisation of such a plan.

Past too is the time when NATO generals and European governments can decide on the establishment of launching-sites and the stockpiling of atomic weapons.

The dangers of atomic war, and its consequences, are now such that these decisions have ceased to be purely matters of politics and can be valid only with the sanction of public opinion.

We live in a time where the good faith of peoples is doubted more than ever before. Expressions throwing doubt on the trustworthiness of each other are bandied back and forth. They are based on what happened in the first world war, when the nations experienced dishonesty, injustice and inhumanity from one another. How can a new trust come about? And it must.

We cannot continue in this paralysing mistrust. If we want to work our way out of the desperate situation in which we find ourselves another spirit must enter into the people. It can only come if the awareness of its necessity suffices to give us strength to believe in its coming. We must presuppose the awareness of this need in all the peoples who have suffered along with us. We must approach them in the spirit that we are human beings, all of us, and that we feel ourselves fitted to feel with each other; to think and to will together in the same way.

The awareness that we are all human beings together has become lost in war and through politics. We have reached the point of regarding each other only as members of a people either allied with us or against us and our approach, prejudice, sympathy or antipathy are all conditioned by that.

Now we must rediscover the fact that we – all together – are human beings, and that we must strive to concede to each other what moral capacity we have. Only in this way can we begin to believe that in other peoples as well as in ourselves there will arise the need for a new spirit, which can be the beginning of a feeling of mutual trustworthiness towards each other.

The spirit is a mighty force for transforming things. We have seen it at work as the spirit of evil which virtually threw us back, from striving towards a culture of the spirit, into barbarism. Now let us set our hopes on the spirit bringing peoples and nations back to an awareness of culture.

At this stage we have the choice of two risks; the one lies in continuing the mad atomic arms race, with its danger of an unavoidable atomic war in the near future; the other in the renunciation of nuclear weapons, and in the hope that the U.S.A. and the Soviet Union and the peoples associated with them, will manage to live in peace. The first holds no hope of a prosperous future; the second does. We must risk the second.

MAN, THE ATOM AND THE RENUNCIATION OF WAR

Professor Max Born has been called the founder of modern physics. A Nobel Prize winner, he was one of 18 German nuclear physicists whose declaration against German atomic weapons rocked Dr. Adenauer's Government. The following statement appeared in the American 'Bulletin of Atomic Scientists' *in June 1957.*

We, the atom and I, have been on friendly terms, until recently.

I saw in it the key to the deepest secrets of Nature, and it revealed to me the greatness of creation and the Creator. It supplied me with satisfactory work, in research and teaching, and thus provided me with a livelihood.

But now it has become the source of deep sorrow and apprehension, to myself as well as to everybody else.

Since the destruction of Nagasaki and Hiroshima the atom has become a spectre threatening us with annihilation. We ourselves have exercised the phantom, it has served us faithfully for a while, but now it is insubordinate.

Would it not be better to have nothing to do with it? Or is it still in our power to tame it and to use it as our servant?

These are the questions which I wish to discuss and try to illuminate: they are fundamental questions for the human race.

I cannot answer them, but I can express a few ideas, some of which the atom itself has taught us; we have to keep these ideas in our minds if we wish to master it.

For the word 'atom' does not stand here for the tiny particle that, when assembled in large numbers, exercises terrible forces, but for the science which has discovered this particle and its collective power.

And the word 'man' not only stands for the rational being that has created atomic science and harnessed atomic power, but also for the man in the street who knows nothing of all that and who reads in his newspapers of a danger which he does not understand.

In fact, it is only a manner of speech to say that the atom has become dangerous, or that the atomic physicists have brought its danger into being. The source of the danger is in all of us, because it is the weakness and passion of ordinary human beings.

Fatal dangers they certainly are: the human race has today the means of annihilating itself – either in a fit of complete lunacy, i.e., in a big war, by a brief fit of destruction, or by careless handling of atomic technology, through a slow process of poisoning and of deterioration in its genetic structure.

The tragic turn was the decision to use the new weapon by dropping two bombs on densely populated Japanese cities.

The justification for the horrible decision which is usually offered is that it speeded up the end of the war and saved the lives of thousands of soldiers, not only Americans but also Japanese.

Not mentioned are the hundreds of thousands of Japanese civilians – men, women and children – who were sacrificed. Or, if they are mentioned, it is said that their destruction was not essentially different from what all belligerents were doing in ordinary air attacks.

And, indeed, nobody can deny this. But can a big crime be justified by the statement that we are accustomed to committing many smaller crimes?

I am not afraid to use the word 'crime', but I shall not call any single person a criminal.

What we are concerned with is collective guilt, the decay of our ethical consciousness, for which we are all to blame, myself included – though I have had nothing to do with the development of nuclear physics.

How little the essence of scientific knowledge has penetrated into men's consciousness was revealed by the period that followed the end of the war.

Many American politicians believed that the technical advantage of the West could be preserved by secrecy.

The effect of this was to hinder the progress of research on their own side and, through the ensuing witch-hunt, to bring about a serious danger to those civil liberties which are the pride of their country. Nothing could prevent the Russians from confirming a known fact of nature and from exploiting it technically.

The explosion of their first uranium bomb in 1949 broke the American monopoly, and when the development of the hydrogen bomb began, the Russians drew level with the West.

The hydrogen bomb is an absolutely devilish invention, and there was opposition to its manufacture in the U.S.A.

The man who had directed the production of the first uranium bomb, Robert Oppenheimer, tried to resist the production of the hydrogen bomb, but without success. He was squeezed out of the Atomic Energy Commission of the American Government.

The principal promoter of the hydrogen bomb was Edward

Teller, who not only developed its theory, but also agitated for its production.

Thus he has inscribed his name in the book of world history – whether on the debit or on the credit side the future will reveal.

Both of these men, Oppenheimer and Teller, as well as Fermi and other participants in this work, including some of the Russian physicists, were once my collaborators in Göttingen long before all these events, at a time when pure science still existed.

It is satisfying to have had such clever and efficient pupils, but I wish they had shown less cleverness and more wisdom.

I feel that I am to blame if all they learned from me were methods of research, and nothing else. Now their cleverness has precipitated the world into a desperate situation.

Both camps, East and West, have a sufficient number of bombs to destroy mutually all big cities and industrial centres with the help of aircraft and of guided and ballistic missiles.

Even the few experimental bombs which have been exploded for 'research' purposes in remote corners of the earth have increased the radioactivity of the atmosphere significantly. After actual nuclear warfare, not much would be left of our civilisation.

The survivors of the bombs would suffer agonising death through radiation sickness; friend and enemy, belligerent and neutral, man, animal and plant.

The leading statesmen of the big atomic Powers are in the habit of declaring that a great war has become impossible. But neither their own foreign offices nor the government of smaller States take much notice of such declarations.

The old diplomatic game, the bargaining and quarrelling about small advantages, continues as if nothing had happened. The reluctance of the Great Powers to be involved in serious conflict is used by smaller nations for blackmail.

East and West are pursuing atomic armament because they distrust one another and are under the illusion that they can gain security by intimidation.

The word 'war' is avoided, but warlike actions, the breaking of international law, and the application of brute force, are perpetrated under other names – as we have recently witnessed in Hungary and in Egypt.

Immensely expensive preparations are constantly being made for a war which must under no circumstances be allowed to come about.

Such is the crazy situation in which we find ourselves. It looks as if our civilisation were condemned to ruin by reason of its own structure.

The literature and philosophy of our time reflect this situation: I am thinking of the novels of Aldous Huxley and George Orwell, and of the writing of existentialist philosophers.

There is no doubt that the human race is in an acute crisis. At the present time, fear alone enforces a precarious peace. However, that is an unstable state of affairs which ought to be replaced by something better.

We do not need to look far in order to find a more solid basis for the proper conduct of our affairs.

It is the principle which is common to all great religions and with which all moral philosophers agree; the principle which in our own part of the world is taught by the doctrine of Christianity; the principle which Mahatma Gandhi had actually carried into practice, before our own eyes, in liberating his own country, India, from foreign domination.

It is the renunciation of force in the pursuit of political aims.

Fifty years ago, when I was young, this statement would have been regarded as utopian and foolish. Today I am able to express it without raising doubts as to my sanity.

It is very likely that tomorrow, not the pacifists, but the bellicose, will be regarded as fools, for the experiences of the last fifty years have left an impact on the minds of men.

Yet I feel unequal to the task of analysing and discussing this immense problem in all its aspects. What would I be able to add to the words of the great poets and prophets of our time?

I have in mind the address given by Albert Schweitzer when he received the Nobel Peace Prize; the declaration published by Albert Einstein, a short time before his death, together with Bertrand Russell and other scholars of many nations; the Mainau manifesto signed by 52 Nobel laureates, and many other similar declarations.

Today these voices no longer die away unheard for the man in the street – and perhaps also some of the great of this world – listen to them.

I am not blind to the difficulties of current policies, the conflict of interests and the clash of ideologies of races, and of religions.

But when in human history have such problems ever been solved by war? Usually, one war has only led to the next one. Is there any possible political aim which would justify the risk of atomic war?

There are a great many politicians and journalists who reply to the warnings of the experts with catch-words such as 'atomic hysteria' and 'bomb defeatism'.

Such politicians and journalists are either shortsighted or fanatics, and therefore evil, or else they represent one of the numerous groups of people to whose advantage it is – or seems to be – that wars be prepared for, or even fought.

Such people are the industrialists who profit from the production of armaments; soldiers who like military life with its romantic tradition, and who prefer blind obedience to personal responsibility; officers, generals, admirals and air marshals whose profession is the preparing and fighting of wars; and, lastly, physicists, chemists and engineers, who invent and manufacture new kinds of weapons.

It is impossible to stabilise the present state of precarious peace based on fear without giving these people other aims in life.

There is no general recipe for doing this. However, I am able to say a few words about the physicists, whose mentality is known to me.

None of them, of course, had the desire to destroy for the sake of fame, but they did wish to contribute to the defence of their own country and of its ideology. They regard as good what is beneficial to their country, just as all other citizens do.

But at the same time they are strongly conscious of a particular mission – and this leads me to a question of supreme importance which I have so far omitted from my consideration.

The discovery of nuclear energy is not only a threat, a danger, to the existence of mankind, but also the means of deep penetration into the secrets of Nature, and thereby of technical progress.

It is, indeed, without exaggeration, the salvation of human civilisation from another creeping danger, namely, the exhaustion of the fossil fuels – coal and oil.

In spite of numerous wars, the number of human beings has increased tremendously during the last 150 years, in a roughly exponential manner, with a doubling period of about 100 years.

Since the total store of fuel is limited, one needs no great gift for prophecy to predict the approach of a fuel crisis for civilised man.

How the long-term problem of the supply of food is to be solved is probably unknown even to the experts in nutrition; but as to the problem of the supply of energy, the discovery of methods for liberating nuclear energy has come just in time to avert a catastrophe.

The atomic physicists are conscious of their responsibility for this development, without which our civilisation would collapse miserably from lack of energy; and they are working devotedly in order to solve the scientific, technological, economic and social problems connected with the new source of energy.

It is as if fate were putting man to the test, saying to us: you want to live, to increase in number, and to improve your conditions – I am giving you the key to your future, but on one condition: that you give up your quarrels, suspicions, and brute force. If you refuse, woe betide you.

Will the warning be heeded?

There are indications that it will. To begin with, amongst the people to whom I professionally belong, the feeling of social responsibility is growing.

In the United States and in Great Britain societies have been formed which oppose the misuse of science for war. The work on the peaceful applications of nuclear physics is being done by international co-operation.

In 1955, a big conference in Geneva was devoted to this purpose, and in 1956 official delegates from many countries met at New York in order to found an international organisation.

I wish to quote a few words from the admirable address given by Niels Bohr to the Geneva meeting:

'It is the very difficulty of appreciating the traditions of other nations on the basis of one's own national tradition that requires that the relationship between cultures may rather be regarded as complementary.'

Free acknowledgement of being different, and replacement of enmity between peoples by the sense of their complementarity: this is the way in which a great abstract thinker urges reconciliation upon the nations before an audience of scientists from all parts of the world.

Amongst Christians, there should be no need for such abstract formulations. It should be sufficient to take the teaching of Christ seriously and to measure good and bad not with a national but with a human gauge.

Never in history was this demand so pressing, never the punishment for refusing it so obvious.

These considerations have naturally led to powerful propaganda for the abolishment of nuclear weapons by international agreement. To be frank, I do not think much of these efforts.

For even if a war between Great Powers should break out and be conducted initially with conventional weapons – with increasing stress, no nation can be expected to renounce the use of any weapon it may see necessary for its salvation.

In fact, military leaders in the U.S.A. have declared they would not wait for extreme emergency, but that in case of attack, they would strike at once against the Eastern bloc with nuclear weapons.

I am convinced that the only way to avoid general destruction is the general renunciation of the use of force in political conflict combined with progressive disarmament.

Instead of the propaganda for the prohibition of atomic weapons, I recommend a vigorous campaign of enlightenment about the nature of total war.

The beautiful idea of the hero who fights and dies for his country, his wife and his child is out of date. Very likely, wife and child will be the victims of the atomic bomb long before the soldier, who is better protected in his dug-out or tank; and the mother country, after being saved from aggression, will look like a landscape on the moon.

Now if we assume that in the future the Great Powers will avoid war, at first from fear, and later perhaps from better motives, and that they will prohibit or at least restrict warlike conflicts between minor nations, what kind of peace will it be?

Hardly a comfortable peace, a paradise on earth, of which I, like many others, have often dreamed. Science and technology will then follow their tendency to rapid expansion unhampered, and in an exponential fashion, until saturation sets in.

But that does not necessarily imply an increase in wealth, still less of happiness, as long as the number of people increases at the same rate, and with it their need for food and energy.

At this point the technical problems of the atom touch social problems, such as birth control and the just distribution of goods. There will be hard fighting about these problems: if not with deadly weapons, then with the more civilised weapons of the mind.

In the background there will always be the danger of self-destruction through the release of nuclear energy, as punishment for relapse into political barbarism.

We have just witnessed with horror such a relapse. For once, we have been saved by the reaction of public opinion throughout the world; public opinion – that means ourselves.

And every one of us can contribute to its becoming more powerful every day.

Stephen King-Hall

REFLECTIONS ON DEFENCE

Commander Sir Stephen King-Hall retired from the Royal Navy in 1929 after serving on the Admiralty naval staff and as Intelligence Officer with the Mediterranean Fleet and Atlantic Fleet. He was a Member of Parliament for Ormskirk, 1939-1945, and founder of the Hansard Society in 1945. The author of several naval and military books, he caused considerable consternation among his colleagues when he began to advocate non-violent methods of defence, first in his own King-Hall News-Letter *and subsequently in a book.* Reflections on Defence *was first published in the newsletter on April 24, 1957. The Defence White Paper referred to is that which argued Mr. Duncan Sandys' concept of massive retaliation with nuclear weapons against even a conventional attack.*

If the defence of the free world can only be secured by physical means it is beyond dispute that the apparatus of defence which the British Government's White Paper on Defence destroys is out of date and beyond our means, and the new machinery foreshadowed in the White Paper is less costly and more likely to be able to do the job.

But the question on which the White Paper is silent is whether physical means are the only or even the best methods of defence.

It is impossible to exaggerate the importance of this question and it seems wholly wrong to assume without any investigation that what may broadly be called military power is the *only* way in which defence can be made effective.

Nor should we be impressed or unduly influenced by the fact that from the earliest known times to the present day, physical force and weapons from the spear to the atom bomb have been the outward and visible signs of defence.

A great many remarkable and unforeseen developments have taken place during the first half of this century and he would have been a bold man who in 1900 would have asserted that within 50 years wireless and television would become principal means of communicating ideas.

Before looking into this matter we should try to answer the question: what is it we are endeavouring to defend? One could argue this at great length but the core of the matter is what is called 'our way of life'. The tension between the West and the Soviet Union is often and correctly described as an ideological struggle. We are desirous of defending an *idea* which is the notion that we should be free to order our lives in accordance with certain practices and principles of a democratic character.

It is assumed that in order to be able to live this way of life we must enjoy national sovereignty and that if we were obliged to accept an alien government (say of a Communist country) we should lose our liberties. This has certainly been true in the past and was manifestly so in days when the victorious conqueror enslaved the whole population or else slaughtered the defeated group and retreated with tangible booty such as women, cattle and solid goods.

Today it is generally recognised that a victorious war cannot be expected to pay a cash dividend. On the contrary the plain fact emerging from two world wars is that after a short period of material suffering the vanquished emerge in a stronger economic position than that of the victors. The victors find themselves in the absurd position, for reasons which appear to be directly in their own interests, of having to finance the recovery of the vanquished and the more complete the physical losses of the enemy the more up-to-date is the new economy which rises from the ashes of defeat.

An interesting and recent example on a small scale of this phenomenon is to be seen in the experiences of the Kikuyu tribe in Kenya. The other tribes are saying with a deal of reason: 'Look at the money and effort which are being expended on social services, rehabilitation, etc., for the Kikuyu. Is it necessary to stage a Mau Mau rebellion in order to receive all these good things?'

An honest answer would be: 'Not necessarily, but it might be helpful!'

There is another relatively new factor in history which must be taken into account.

We seem to have reached a stage in military evolution in which resistance, both passive and active, of a civilian population which refuses to acknowledge defeat even though its professional forces have been defeated or because it had no conventional forces to be defeated, is a new factor in war.

Gandhi's passive resistance campaign in India; the German passive resistance which defeated the French in the Ruhr in the 1920s; the Sinn Fein nationally supported terrorist campaign; the Israel victory over the British mandatory administration; the Algerian struggle; the EOKA movement in Cyprus; the resistance movements against the Nazis, all belong to this new development.

It seems to be of significance that all these 'civilian' resistances were part of ideological struggles and illustrated the truth of the saying that one can do most things with bayonets except sit on them.

Tentative conclusions are as follows:

(1) We aim to defend an *idea.*

(2) There are some grounds for believing that an *idea* can prevail even when the opponents of the idea are physically superior and able to occupy the territory of those defending the *idea.*

(3) In the modern world a military victory cannot produce an economic dividend. Still less can there be any profit in a military victory obtained by nuclear weapons.

As mentioned above it is generally taken for granted that the basis of defence against agression must be military force. We have however reached an unprecedented state of affairs in the evolution of destructive force through the invention of nuclear weapons.

They possess two characteristics which are novel.

The first is that their destructive capacity is so enormous that there is no practical physical means of defence against these weapons.

This fact has been self-evident so far as the U.K. is concerned for several years but is now officially accepted.

The second novel characteristic of these weapons is that each time one of them is tested there is an addition to the pollution of the earth's surface and atmosphere.

Although the whole subject of fall-out and the strontium risk is a matter of scientific controversy there is agreement that if tests were carried out over a long period on a large scale the human race would probably exterminate itself in preparing to defend itself.

The peculiar character of the nuclear weapon has given a very real meaning to the hallowed principle that all nations maintain defence forces for protection against aggression. In the pre-nuclear age it was always said that the purpose of armed forces was to prevent war and there was some truth in the statement but the use of the word ' deterrent ' and the idea it expresses is a product of the nuclear age. It is insufficiently appreciated that our defence strategy is now based on the belief or hope that an *idea* will be effective and the *idea* can be summarised as follows:

' Nuclear war would be mutual suicide. It is not rational to be suicidal. You – the aggressor – can destroy us but your own destruction will be practically coincidental.'

Unfortunately as I once pointed out this theoretical argument may not be completely valid when applied to the particular case of the free world versus the Soviet Union for the following reasons.

(1) Can we assume that the vulnerability of the U.K.-U.S.A.-Western Europe target is not greater than that of the Russian target? There are in my judgment reasons for fearing that there is a disbalance here. So far as the U.K. is concerned it has been authoritatively said that ten H-bombs of the Megaton size would reduce the country to chaotic ruin with millions of casualties. I find it hard to believe that a similar effect could be produced in the huge areas of the Soviet Union. We assume that the principal cities and industrial areas of the Soviet Union including the oil fields could be smashed, but this would not obliterate the Russian State. A peasant economy would continue to survive.

(2) We are in the dilemma, which is one of the penalties of being democratic, that even in an acute crisis we cannot be the first to strike and this is particularly true in the case of launching a nuclear attack.

(3) Is there not a danger that the Russians might gamble on the chance that if they launch an attack its devastating consequences would cripple the counter-attack? If one thinks this out we are in the strange position that *at the best* a small number of persons (the Government, whom we assume would be 70 feet underground) and the bomber force (or in a few years' time the guided missile crews) would, a few hours after the Russian nuclear attack, be the only organised part of the nation! They would presumably launch the counter-attack and inflict fearful damage on the Russians.

It has never been very clear to me what benefit the millions of dead and dying in Britain would derive from this operetion. When the nuclear attack was limited to the relatively small atomic bombs the conception of the broken-backed war made sense. But the H-bomb has blown the foundations out of that theory. One cannot have a broken-backed war if, instead of the joints of the back-bone being dislocated, the vertebrae are disintegrated.

The White Paper on Defence says cautiously: 'It may well be that the initial nuclear bombardment *and counter-bombardment* by aircraft or rockets would be so crippling as to bring the war to an end within a few weeks or even days.' (Para 24.) The italics are mine.

If one thinks this out one is forced to the conclusion that, bearing in mind the implication in the statement that we are not to initiate the bombardment but only the counter-bombardment, the war for all practical purposes so far as the U.K. were concerned would be at an end without the counter-bombardment. Indeed if one is to be absolutely realistic about this matter and think in terms of the long-range future of the human race and accept the virtual certainty that the Russia of AD 2000 will not resemble that of 1955 we must consider two possible contingencies:

(a) A state of affairs in which the U.K. is devastated but Russia is not because for one reason or other the counter-attack is not launched.

(b) A state of affairs in which the U.K. and Russia are both devastated.

Are we certain that in terms of the long-range future of the human race (b) is preferable to (a)?

I will not repeat other qualifying reflections about the efficacy of the deterrent but will summarise two of them:

(a) If the deterrent idea works then we are back to conventional warfare. It has been argued for example that in World War II gas or bacteriological methods of war were not used because neither side could see how to do so advantageously. But if we exclude nuclear warfare then there is unfortunately no doubt whatsoever that on sea, in the air and on land the Russian forces are overwhelmingly stronger than those of NATO and likely to remain so.

(b) To make up for this fact we have announced that we shall use nuclear weapons tactically. We have shown elsewhere that the distinction between tactical and strategical nuclear weapons is meaningless and that a ‘ tactical ’ use develops inevitably into strategical nuclear war. Nor do I see on what grounds it can be assumed that the Russians will not own and employ tactical nuclear weapons.

The arguments and facts set forth here lead to the conclusion that the time-honoured theory that defence against physical aggression must take the form of physical means has worn very thin and needs to be regarded with much suspicion.

Moreover experience has shown that aggression by the Communist States can also be political and since 1945 this form of aggression has been the most dangerous and insidious. Para. 27 of the White Paper on Defence writes about British responsibilities under the Bagdad Pact to *prevent Communist encroachment and infiltration* and goes on in the same paragraph to refer to *bomber squadrons based in Cyprus capable of delivering nuclear weapons.* The value of nuclear bombardments as a means of preventing (say) a Communist *coup d'état* in Persia is not clear to this writer.

Finally there is a theoretical or philosophic reason for doubting whether military force is any longer assuredly the best way to counter military aggression of a nuclear type. It is an established principle that to every form of attack there must exist a means of defence. We have now reached a stage in the development of the attack which enables total destruction to be achieved and as it is physically impossible to put the whole of a modern social system 100 feet underground and turn the United Kingdom into a nation of troglodytes it might seem at first glance that the principle has broken down.

But it seems to have been forgotten that the principle does not say that the answer to an attack must be of *the same order of things as the attack.*

If the answer to a nuclear attack creating total destruction is merely to enlarge the area of destruction nothing of value has been achieved.

If however having reached the *ne plus ultra* of physical attack we are imaginative enough to realise that we have not simultaneously reached the frontiers of human thought we should have no difficulty in moving forward beyond the physical into the psychological. Let us see where such an exploratory journey might lead us.

I invite the reader to put on one side all his preconceived notions about defence and start from the simple proposition that we desire to defend our way of life and would prefer not to do it by risking its utter destruction.

Our way of life is menaced at this time by the actions and threats of the Communist powers. These actions and threats are the consequences of ideas and thoughts in the minds of the rulers of Russia.

We have good reason to believe that the men in the Kremlin wish to destroy our way of life. Why?

It is important to make an attempt to pin-point why the Russian Government wishes to destroy us. There is probably more than one reason and the following include the most likely ones:

(1) Fear that it is the ultimate purpose of the Western powers to overthrow the Russian Government by force. Linked with this may be fear that Germans will exact revenge and reconquer lost territories.

(2) A missionary urge to spread Communism. We doubt whether this is really very powerful. It seems more likely that today the Communist creed is a convenient weapon in the armoury of Russian power politics of a nationalist character.

(3) Fear that the principles and practices of the free world will subvert the loyalty of the Russian people to the Communist regime.

These are guesses and we must stress the extreme importance from the point of view of the new theory of defence we are submitting for discussion of making every effort to ascertain accurately the psychological explanation which accounts for the hostile attitude towards the free world of those who at this time control the resources of the Russian people.

For it is the essence of a defensive strategy which seeks security for the way of life it is designed to defend by operating in the field of ideas, that there should be accurate information about the nature of the ideas which breed an aggressive attitude.

However in default of the existence of better information which could probably be obtained if a substantial effort to do so was made by the free world, let us suppose that the three reasons given above contain at any rate some of the truth.

Now the object of the new strategy of defence is to change the minds of the men in the Kremlin.

To those who will at once raise the cry that this is asking the impossible the reply must be:

(a) They are human beings who have for one reason or another changed their minds on several occasions since 1945.

(b) Through the policy of the nuclear deterrent we hope – and some people believe – we are already operating on their minds and influencing their thoughts. If we are not the deterrent idea has failed.

If our strategy should be to change the minds of the men in the Kremlin how is this to be achieved tactically? There seems to us to be two broad lines of aproach; the direct and the indirect.

The direct approach consists in doing things which might make an immediate impact on the minds of the rulers; the indirect approach is composed of policies designed to influence the minds of the masses in the Communist-controlled countries.

At this moment we are disposed to think that as part of our psychological campaign for defence there are strong arguments for considering whether the U.K. should not announce unilaterally that it will *not* carry out any further tests and that the forthcoming test will be abandoned.

Something dramatic and easily understood by mankind needs to be done to break the deadlock and arrest the drift to disaster.

Do the chiefs of staff really believe that an announcement of this nature would leave the U.K. more defenceless against nuclear attack than it is at present?

Are we to suppose – assuming the deterrent idea to be better than we believe it to be – that the Americans have not sufficient H- and A-bombs for use on behalf of the free world? If we have some know-how exclusively British, give it to the Americans.

Having taken this step we should use it as the starting point for a tremendous and world-wide educational campaign explaining the horrors of nuclear war, the dangers of tests, etc., and say: 'Now you can see why Her Majesty's Government has taken a lead and perhaps risks in this matter.'

I picture a sum of £100,000,000 being spent on this propaganda which ought to be an all-party effort. I refuse absolutely to admit that given imagination, energy and funds the great educational campaign should not penetrate beyond the iron curtain.

In this connection and beginning with the satellite States a really great effort (£50,000,000) should be made to increase contacts with the masses in those countries. Every effort should be made to organise exchange visits between young people on a very large scale. We should put as much effort and money into this kind of thing as we do into a nuclear-bomb test.

No doubt these ideas will be very startling to many people but we beg and entreat them to remember that we are faced today with the old problem of defence in a completely novel setting.

It is almost as novel as if we woke up one day to find that this world of ours was liable to aggression from another planet. Our present problem is of this novel nature. I said recently that the White Paper was a good bite at half the cherry. The argument that a very large part of our defence expenditure and effort should be concentrated on the field of political warfare takes us into three-quarters of the cherry. What about the rest of it?

The 'Guardian' wrote on April 15 that 'Dependence on the ultimate deterrent is inevitable.' It went on to say that the alternative was 'conventional forces on a massive scale' or 'a fully pacifist policy.' A point worth thinking about is that *if* we succeed in producing some form of stand-still in development of nuclear weapons and do *not* succeed in making progress with disarmament in conventional weapons are we likely to be able to persuade the people of the West to stand the racket of 'conventional forces on a massive scale?' We doubt it.

What about a fully pacifist policy?

The truth is that this possibility has never been thoroughly examined from a strictly political–strategical angle. The 'pacifist' policy has usually been defended from a moral point of view.

I am thinking of a policy which it would be more accurate to call 'defence by passive resistance.'

I am not saying it would work. I am saying that no one has thoroughly studied its possibilities in the light of the novel and unprecedented defence problem which now faces the U.K., Western Europe and to a lesser extent the U.S.A.

This may be the remaining quarter of the cherry.

In order to find out some more about this I have reached the conclusion that a Royal Commission should be established with the task of expressing an opinion upon the problem of whether our way of life could be defended by passive resistance and if so what the plan should be. If a Royal Commission is not considered to be the best instrument then a special committee of the Imperial Defence College should be put on the job.

We have said quite bluntly in the White Paper that we cannot afford our present expenditure on defence. We have made heavy cuts in our conventional forces and transferred our faith to nuclear weapons with all the imponderables and unknowns which go with them.

I remarked to a well-known MP: ' Suppose Great Britain only had three air-borne divisions, a few tactical aircraft and a very small navy, what would happen apart from the obvious and immense gain to our economy?'

He replied: ' My first reflection is that our influence in the world would at once decline ' – he paused and added – ' at least I suppose it would.'

Is this certain? Gandhi's influence rose with the rise of passive resistance; so did that of the African bus boycotters.

Has it or can it be proved that a United Kingdom with an intelligent and sophisticated population educated to regard a national plan of passive resistance as the defence policy of the country would lose influence? I think there is a case for a very thorough investigation of this matter.

James Kirkup

NO MORE HIROSHIMAS

'Peace News', *August 5, 1960*

At the station exit, my bundle in hand,
Early the winter afternoon's wet snow
Falls thinly round me, out of a crudded sun.
I had forgotten to remember where I was.
Looking about, I see it might be anywhere –
A station, a town like any other in Japan,
Ramshackle, muddy, noisy, drab; a cheerfully
Shallow permanence: peeling concrete, litter, ' Atomic
Lotion, for hair fall-out,' a flimsy department-store;
Racks and towers of neon, flashy over tiled and tilted waves
Of little roofs, shacks cascading lemons and persimmons,
Oranges and dark-red apples, shanties awash with rainbows
Of squid and octopus, shellfish, slabs of tuna, oysters, ice,
Ablaze with fans of soiled nude-picture books
Thumbed abstractedly by schoolboys, with second-hand looks.

The river remains unchanged, sad, refusing re-habilitation.
In this long, wide, empty, official boulevard
The new trees are still small, the office blocks
Basely functional, the bridge a slick abstraction.
But the river remains unchanged, sad, refusing re-habilitation.

In the city centre, far from the station's lively squalor,
A kind of life, goes on, in cinemas and hi-fi coffee bars,
In the shuffling racket of pin-table palaces and parlours,
The souvenir-shops piled with junk, kimonoed kewpie-dolls,
Models of the bombed Industry Promotion Hall, memorial ruin,
Trickled out with glitter-frost and artificial pearls.

Set in an awful emptiness, the modern tourist hotel is trimmed
With jaded Christmas frippery, flatulent balloons; in the hall,
A giant dingy iced cake in the shape of a Cinderella coach.
The contemporary stairs are treacherous, the corridors
Deserted, my room an overheated morgue, the bar in darkness.
Punctually, the electric chimes ring out across the tidy waste
Their doleful public hymn – the tune unrecognisable, evangelist.

Here atomic peace is geared to meet the tourist trade.
Let it remain like this, for all the world to see,
Without nobility or loveliness, and dogged with shame
That is beyond all hope of indignation. Anger, too, is dead.
And why should memorials of what was far
From pleasant have the grace that helps us to forget?

In the dying afternoon, I wander dying round the Park of Peace.
It is right, this squat, dead place, with its left-over air
Of an abandoned International Trade and Tourist Fair.

The stunted trees are wrapped in straw against the cold.
The gardeners are old, old women in blue bloomers, white aprons,
Survivors weeding the dead brown lawns around the Children's
Monument.

A hideous pile, the Atomic Bomb Explosion Centre, freezing cold,
'Includes the Peace Tower, a museum containing
Atomic-melted slates and bricks, photos showing
What the Atomic Desert looked like, and other
Relics of the catastrophe.'

The other relics:
The ones that made me weep;
The bits of burnt clothing,
The stopped watches, the torn shirts,
The twisted buttons,
The stained and tattered vests and drawers,
The ripped kimonos and charred boots,
The white blouse polka-dotted with atomic rain, indelible,
The cotton summer pants the blasted boys crawled home in to
bleed
And slowly die.

Remember only these.
They are the memorials we need.

J. B. Priestley

BRITAIN AND THE NUCLEAR BOMBS

J. B. Priestley's Britain and the Nuclear Bombs *appeared in* ' The New Statesman ' *on November 2 1957.*

Two events of this autumn should compel us to reconsider the question of Britain and the nuclear bombs. The first of these events was Mr Aneurin Bevan's speech at the Labour Party conference, which seemed to many of us to slam a door in our faces. It was not dishonest but it was very much a party conference speech, and its use of terms like ' unilateral ' and ' polarisation ' lent it a suggestion of the ' Foreign Office spokesman '. Delegates asked not to confuse ' an emotional spasm ' with ' statesmanship ' might have retorted that the statesmanship of the last ten years has produced little else but emotional spasms. And though it is true, as Mr Bevan argued, that independent action by this country, to ban nuclear bombs, would involve our foreign minister in many difficulties, most of us would rather have a bewildered and overworked Foreign Office than a country about to be turned into a radio-active cemetery. Getting out of the water may be difficult but it is better than drowning.

The second event was the successful launching of the Soviet satellite, followed by an immediate outbreak of what may fairly be called *satellitis,* producing a rise in temperature and signs of delirium. In the poker game, where Britain still sits, nervously fingering a few remaining chips, like a Treasury official playing with two drunk oil millionaires, the stakes have been doubled again. Disarmament talks must now take place in an atmosphere properly belonging to boys' papers and science fiction, though already charged with far more hysterical competitiveness. If statesmanship is to see us through, it will have to break the familiar and dubious pattern of the last few years. Perhaps what we need now, before it is too late, is not statesmanship but lifemanship.

One ' ultimate weapon ', the final deterrent, succeeds another. After the bombs, the inter-continental rockets; and after the rockets, according to the First Lord of the Admiralty, the guided-missile submarine, which will ' carry a guided missile with a nuclear war-head and appear off the coast of any country in the world with a capability of penetrating to the centre of any continent.' The prospect now is not of countries without navies but of navies without countries. And we have arrived at an insane regress of ultimate weapons that are not ultimate.

But all this is to the good; and we cannot have too much of it, we are told, because no men in their right minds would let loose such powers of destruction. Here is the realistic view. Any criticism of it is presumed to be based on wild idealism. But surely it is the wildest idealism, at the furthest remove from a sober realism, to assume that men will always behave reasonably and in line with their best interests? Yet this is precisely what we are asked to believe, and to stake our all on it.

For that matter, why should it be assumed that the men who create and control such monstrous devices *are* in their right minds? They live in an unhealthy mental climate, an atmosphere dangerous to sanity. They are responsible to no large body of ordinary sensible men and women, who pay for these weapons without ever having ordered them, who have never been asked anywhere yet if they wanted them. When and where have these preparations for nuclear warfare ever been put to the test of public opinion? We cannot even follow the example of the young man in the limerick and ask *Who does what and with which and to whom?* The whole proceedings take place in the stifling secrecy of an expensive lunatic asylum. And as one ultimate weapon after another is added to the pile, the mental climate deteriorates, the atmosphere thickens, and the tension is such that soon something may snap.

The more elaborately involved and hair-triggered the machinery of destruction, the more likely it is that this machinery will be set in motion, if only by accident. Three glasses too many of vodka or bourbon-on-the-rocks, and the wrong button may be pushed. Combine this stock-piling of nuclear weapons with a crazy competitiveness boastful confidence in public and a mounting fear in private, and what was unthinkable a few years ago now at the best only seems unlikely and very soon may seem inevitable. Then western impatience cries 'Let's get the damned thing over!' and eastern fatalism mutters 'If this has to be, then we must accept it.' And people in general are now in a worse position every year, further away from intervention; they have less and less freedom of action; they are deafened and blinded by propaganda and giant headlines; they are robbed of decision by fear or apathy.

It is possible, as some thinkers hold, that our civilisation is bent on self-destruction, hurriedly planning its own doomsday. This may explain, better than any wearisome recital of plot and counter-plot in terms of world power, the curious, sinister air of somnambulism there is about our major international affairs, the steady drift from bad to worse, the speeches that begin to sound meaningless, the conferences that achieve nothing, all the persons of great consequence who somehow seem like puppets. We have all known people in whom was sown the fatal seed of self-destruction, people who would sit with us making sensible plans and then go off and quietly bring them to nothing, never really looking for anything but death. Our industrial civilisation, behaving in a similar fashion, may be under the same kind of spell, hell-bent on murdering itself. But it is possible that the spell can be broken. If it can, then it will only be by an immensely decisive gesture, a clear act of will. Instead of endless bargaining for a little of this in exchange for a little of that, while all the time the bargainers are being hurried down a road that gets steeper and narrower, somebody will have to say 'I'm through with all this.'

In plain words: now that Britain has told the world she has the H-bomb she should announce as early as possible that she has done with it, that she proposes to reject, in all circumstances, nuclear warfare. This is not pacifism. There is no suggestion here of abandoning the immediate defence of this island. Indeed, it might well be considerably strengthened, reducing the threat of actual invasion, which is the root fear in people's minds, a fear often artfully manipulated for purposes far removed from any defence of hearth and home. (This is of course the exact opposite of the views expressed at the Tory conference by Mr. Sandys, who appears to believe that bigger and bigger bombs and rockets in more and more places, if necessary, thousands of miles away, will bring us peace and prosperity). No, what should be abandoned is the idea of deterrence-by-threat-of-retaliation. There is no real security in it, no decency in it, no faith, hope, nor charity in it.

But let us take a look at our present policy entirely on its own low level. There is no standing still, no stalemates, in this idiot game; one 'ultimate weapon' succeeds another. To stay in the race at all, except in an ignominious position, we risk bankruptcy, the disappearance of the Welfare State, a standard of living that might begin to make Communist propaganda sound more attractive than it does at present. We could in fact be so busy, inspired by the indefatigable Mr Sandys, defending ourselves against Communism somewhere else, a long way off, that we could wake up one morning to hear it knocking on the back door. Indeed, this is Moscow's old *heads-I-win-tails-you-lose* policy.

Here we might do well to consider western world strategy, first grandiloquently proclaimed by Sir Winston in those speeches he made in America just after the war. The Soviet Union was to be held in leash by nuclear power. We had the bomb and they hadn't. The race would be on but the West had a flying start. But Russia was not without physicists, and some German scientists and highly trained technicians had disappeared somewhere in eastern Europe. For the immediate defence of West Germany, the atom bomb threat no doubt served its turn. But was this really sound long-term strategy? It created the unhealthy climate, the poisonous atmosphere of our present time. It set the Russians galloping in the nuclear race. It freed them from the immense logistic problems that must be solved if large armies are to be moved everywhere, and from some very tricky problems of morale that would soon appear once the Red Army was a long way from home. It encouraged the support of so-called peoples' and nationalistic and anti-colonial wars, not big enough to be settled by nuclear weapons. In spite of America's ring of advanced air bases, the race had only to be run a little longer to offer Russia at least an equally good set-up, and, in comparison with Britain alone, clearly an enormously better set-up.

We are like a man in a poker game who never dare cry 'I'll see you.' The Soviet Union came through the last war because it had vast spaces and a large population and a ruthless disregard of losses, human and material. It still has them. Matched against this overcrowded island with its intricate urban organisation, at the last dreadful pinch – and party dictators made to feel unsure of their power can pinch quicker than most democratic leaders – the other side possesses all the advantages. If there is one country that should never have gambled in this game, it is Britain. Once the table stakes were being raised, the chips piling up, we were out. And though we may have been fooling ourselves, we have not been fooling anybody else.

This answers any gobbling cries about losing our national prestige. We have none, in terms of power. (The world has still respect and admiration for our culture, and we are busy reducing that respect and admiration by starving it. The cost of a few bombs might have made all the difference.) We ended the war high in the world's regard. We could have taken over its moral leadership, spoken and acted for what remained of its conscience; but we chose to act otherwise – with obvious and melancholy consequences both abroad, where in power politics we cut a shabby figure, and at home, where we shrug it away or all go to the theatre to applaud the latest jeers and sneers at Britannia. It has been said we cannot send our ministers naked to the conference table. But the sight of a naked minister might bring to the conference some sense of our human situation. What we do is something much worse: we send them there half-dressed, half-smart, half-tough, half-apologetic, figures inviting contempt. That is why we are so happy and excited when we can send abroad a good-looking young woman in a pretty new dress to represent us, playing the only card we feel can take a trick – the Queen.

It is argued, as it was most vehemently by Mr Bevan at Brighton, that if we walked out of the nuclear arms race then the world would be ' polarised ' between America and the Soviet Union, without any hope of mediation between the two fixed and bristling camps. ' Just consider for a moment,' he cried, ' all the little nations running, one here and one there, one running to Russia, the other to the U.S., all once more clustering under the castle wall . . .' But surely this is one of those ' realistic ' arguments that are not based on reality. The idea of the Third Force was rejected by the very party Mr Bevan was addressing. The world was polarised when, without a single protest from all the noisy guardians of our national pride, parts of East Anglia ceased to be under our control and became an American air base. We cannot at one and the same time be both an independent power, bargaining on equal terms, and a minor ally or satellite. If there are little nations that do not run for shelter to the walls of the White House or the Kremlin because they are happy to accept Britain as their nuclear umbrella, we hear very little about them. If it is a question of brute power, this argument is unreal.

It is not entirely stupid, however, because something more than brute power is involved. There is nothing unreal in the idea of a third nation, especially one like ours, old and experienced in world affairs, possessing great political traditions, to which other and smaller nations could look while the two new giants mutter and glare at each other. But it all depends what that nation is doing. If it is still in the nuclear gamble, without being able to control or put an end to the game, then the nation is useless to others, is frittering its historical prestige, and the polarisation, which Mr Bevan sees as the worst result of our rejection of nuclear warfare, is already an accomplished fact. And if it is, then we must ask ourselves what we can do to break this polarity, what course of action on our part might have some hope of changing the world situation. To continue doing what we are doing will not change it. Even during the few weeks since Mr Bevan made his speech the world is becoming more rigidly and dangerously polarised than ever, just because the Russians have sent a metal football circling the globe. What then can Britain do to de-polarise the world?

The only move left that can mean anything is to go into reverse, decisively rejecting nuclear warfare. This gives the world something quite different from the polarised powers: there is now a country that can make H-bombs but decides against them. Had Britain taken this decision some years ago the world would be a safer and saner place than it is today. But it is still not too late. And such a move will have to be 'unilateral'; doomsday may arrive before the nuclear powers reach any agreement; and it is only a decisive 'unilateral' move that can achieve the moral force it needs to be effective.

It will be a hard decision to take because all habit is against it. Many persons of consequence and their entourages of experts would have to think fresh thoughts. They would have to risk losing friends and not influencing people. For example, so far as they involve nuclear warfare, our commitments to Nato, Seato and the rest and our obligations to the Commonwealth, would have to be sharply adjusted. Anywhere from Brussels to Brisbane, reproaches would be hurled, backs would be turned. But what else have these countries to suggest, what way out, what hope for man? And if, to save our souls and this planet, we are willing to remain here and take certain risks, why should we falter because we might have complaints from Rhodesia and reproaches from Christchurch, N.Z.? And it might not be a bad idea if the Nato peoples armed themselves to defend themselves, taking their rifles to the ranges at the week-end, like the Swiss.

American official and service opinion would be dead against us, naturally. The unsinkable (but expendable) aircraft carrier would have gone. Certain Soviet bases allotted to British nuclear attack would have to be included among the targets of the American Strategic Air Service. And so on and so forth. But though service chiefs and their staffs go on examining and marking the maps and planning their logistics, having no alternative but resignation, they are as fantastic and unreal in their way as their political and diplomatic colleagues are in theirs. What is fantastic and unreal is their assumption that they are traditionally occupied with their professional duties, attending in advance to the next war, Number Three in the world series. But what will happen – and one wrong report by a sleepy observer might start it off – will not be anything recognisable as a war, an affair of victories and defeats, something that one side can win or that you can call off when you have had enough. It will be universal catastrophe and apocalypse, the crack of doom into which Communism, western democracy, their way of life and our way of life, may disappear for ever. And it is not hard to believe that this is what some of our contemporaries really desire, that behind their photogenic smiles and cheerful patter nothing exists but the death wish.

We live in the thought of this prospect as if we existed in a permanent smog. All sensible men and women – and this excludes most of those who are in the *V.I.P.-Highest-Priority-Top-Secret-Top-People Class,* men now so conditioned by this atmosphere of power politics, intrigue, secrecy, insane invention, that they are more than half-barmy – have no illusions about what is happening to us. and know that those responsible have made two bad miscalculations. First, they have prostituted so much science in the preparations for war that they have completely changed the character of what they are doing, without any equivalent change in the policies of and relations between states. Foreign affairs, still conducted as if the mobilisation of a few divisions might settle something, are now backed with push-button arrangements to let loose earthquakes and pestilences and pronounce the death sentences of continents. This leaves us all in a worse dilemma than the sorcerer's apprentice. The second miscalcultaion assumed that if the odds were only multiplied fast enough, your side would break through because the other side would break down. And because this has not happened, a third illusion is being welcomed, namely, that now, with everything piling up, poker chips flung on the table by the handful, the tension obviously increasing, now at last we are arriving at an acknowledged drawn game, a not-too-stale stalemate, a cosy old balance of power. This could well be the last of our illusions.

The risk of our rejecting nuclear warfare, totally and in all circumstances, is quite clear, all too easy to understand. We lose such bargaining power as we now possess. We have no deterrent to a nuclear threat. We deliberately exchange 'security' for insecurity. (And the fact that some such exchange is recommended by the major religions, in their earlier and non-establishment phases, need not detain us here.) But the risk is clear and the arguments against running it quite irrefutable, only if we refuse, as from the first too many of us here have refused, to take anything but short-term conventional views, only if we will not follow any thought to its conclusion. Our 'hard-headed realism' is neither hard-headed nor realistic just because it insists on our behaving in a new world as if we were still living in an old world, the one that has been replaced.

Britain runs the greatest risk by just mumbling and muddling along, never speaking out, avoiding any decisive creative act. For a world in which our deliberate 'insecurity' would prove to be our undoing is not a world in which real security could be found. As the game gets faster, the competition keener, the unthinkable will turn into the inevitable, the weapons will take command, and the deterrents will not deter. Our bargaining power is slight; the force of our example might be great. The catastrophic antics of our time have behind them men hag-ridden by fear, which explains the neurotic irrationality of it all, the crazy disproportion between means and ends. If we openly challenge this fear then we might break the wicked spell that all but a few uncertified lunatics desperately wish to see broken, we could begin to restore the world to sanity and lift this nation from its recent ignominy to its former grandeur. Alone, we defied Hitler; and alone we can defy this nuclear madness into which the spirit of Hitler seems to have passed, to poison the world. There may be other chain-reactions besides those leading to destruction; and we might start one. The British of these times, so frequently hiding their decent, kind faces behind masks of sullen apathy or sour, cheap cynicism, often seem to be waiting for something better than party squabbles and appeals to their narrowest self interest, something great and noble in its intention that would make them feel good again. And this might well be a declaration to the world that after a certain date one power able to engage in nuclear warfare will reject the evil thing for ever.

Bertrand Russell

AN OPEN LETTER TO EISENHOWER AND KRUSHCHEV

Bertrand Russell's open letter to Eisenhower and Krushchev, published in ' The New Statesman ' *on November 23 1957, attracted so much attention that Krushchev and United States Secretary of State Mr. John Foster Dulles subsequently replied, to justify their policies. This was Russell's first venture into the field of direct diplomacy.*

MOST POTENT SIRS,

I am addressing you as the respective heads of the two most powerful countries in the world. Those who direct the policies of these countries have a power for good or evil exceeding anything ever possessed before by any man or group of men. Public opinion in your respective countries has been focused upon the points in which your national interests are thought to diverge, but I am convinced that you, as far-seeing and intelligent men, must be aware that the matters in which the interest of Russia and America coincide are much more important than the matters in which they are thought to diverge. I believe that if you two eminent men were jointly to proclaim this fact and to bend the policies of your great countries to agreement with such proclamation, there would be throughout the world, and not least in your own countries, a shout of joyful agreement which would raise you both to a pinnacle of fame surpassing anything achieved by other statesmen of the past or present. Although you are, of course, both well aware of the points in which the interests of Russia and America are identical, I will, for the sake of explicitness, enumerate some of them.

(1) The supreme concern of men of all ways of thought at the present time must be to ensure the continued existence of the human race. This is already in jeopardy from the hostility between East and West and will, if many minor nations acquire nuclear weapons, be in very much greater jeopardy within a few years from the possibilty of irresponsible action by thoughtless fanatics.

Some ignorant militarists, both in the east and in the west, have apparently thought that the danger could be averted by a world war giving victory to their own side. The progress of science and technology has made this an idle dream. A world war would not result in the victory of either side, but in the extermination of both. Neither side can desire such a cataclysm.

The hope of world dominion, either military or ideological, is one which has hovered before many men in the past and has led invariably to disaster. Philip II of Spain made the attempt and reduced his country to the status of a minor power. Louis XIV of France made the attempt and by exhausting his country led the way to the French Revolution, which he would have profoundly deplored. Hitler, in our own day, fought for the world-wide supremacy of the Nazi philosophy, and perished miserably. Two great men propounded ideologies which have not yet run their course: I mean the authors of the Declaration of Independence and the Communist Manifesto. There is no reason to expect that either of these ideologies will be more successful in conquering the world than their predecessors, Buddhist, Christian, Moslem, or Nazi. What is new in the present situation is not the impossibility of success, but the magnitude of the disaster which must result from the attempt. We must, therefore, hope that each side will abandon the futile strife and agree to allow to each a sphere proportionate to its present power.

(2) The international anarchy which will inevitably result from the unrestricted diffusion of nuclear weapons is not to the interest of either Russia or America. There was a time when only America had nuclear weapons. This was followed by a time when only Russia and America had such weapons. And now only Russia, America and Britain possess them. It is obvious that, unless steps are taken, France and Germany will shortly manufacture these weapons. It is not likely that China will lag far behind. We must expect that during the next few years the manufacture of engines of mass destruction will become cheaper and easier. No doubt Egypt and Israel will then be able to follow the example set by the great powers. So will the states of South America. There is no end to this process until every sovereign state is in a position to say to the whole world: 'You must yield to my demands or you shall die.' If all sovereign states were governed by rulers possessed of even the rudiments of sanity, they would be restrained from such blackmail by the fear that their citizens also would perish. But experience shows that from time to time power in this or that country falls into the hands of rulers who are not sane. Can anyone doubt that Hitler, if he had been able to do so, would have chosen to involve all mankind in his own ruin? For such reasons, it is imperative to put a stop to the diffusion of nuclear weapons. This can easily be done by agreement between Russia and America, since they can jointly refuse

military or economic assistance to any country other than themselves which persists in the manufacture of such weapons. But it cannot be achieved without agreement between the two dominant powers, for, without such agreement, each new force of nuclear weapons will be welcomed by one side or the other as an increase to its own strength. This helter-skelter race towards ruin must be stopped if anything that anybody could desire is to be effected.

(3) So long as the fear of world war dominates policy and the only deterrent is the threat of universal death, so long there can be no limit to the diversion of expenditure of funds and human energy into channels of destruction. It is clear that both Russia and the U.S.A. could save nine-tenths of their present expenditure if they concluded an alliance and devoted themselves jointly to the preservation of peace throughout the world. If they do not find means of lessening their present hostility, reciprocal fear will drive them further and further, until, apart from immense armaments, nothing beyond a bare subsistence will be left to the populations of either country. In order to promote efficiency in the preparation of death, education will have to be distorted and stunted. Everything in human achievement that is not inspired by hatred and fear will be squeezed out of the curriculum in schools and universities. Any attempt to preserve the vision of Man as the triumph (so far) of the long ages of evolution, will come to be viewed as treachery, since it will be thought not to minister to the victory of this group or that. Such a prospect is death to the hopes of all who share the aspirations which have inspired human progress since the dawn of history.

(4) I cannot but think that you would both rejoice if a way could be found to disperse the pall of fear which at present dims the hopes of mankind. Never before, since our remote ancestors descended from the trees, has there been valid reason for such fear. Never before has such a sense of futility blighted the visions of youth. Never before has there been reason to feel that the human race was travelling along a road ending only in a bottomless precipice. Individual death we must all face, but collective death has never, hitherto, been a grim possibility.

And, all this fear, all this despair, all this waste is utterly unnecessary. One thing only is required to dispel the darkness and enable the world to live again in a noon-day brightness of hope. The one thing necessary is that East and West should recognise their respective rights, admit that each must learn to live with the other and substitute argument for force in the attempt to spread their respective ideologies. It is not necessary that either side should abandon belief in its own creed. It is only necessary that it should abandon the attempt to spread its own creed by force of arms.

I suggest, Sirs, that you should meet in a frank discussion of the conditions of co-existence, endeavouring no longer to secure this or that more or less surreptitious advantage for your own side, but seeking rather for such agreements and such adjustments in the world as will diminish future occasions of strife. I believe that if you were to do this the world would acclaim your action, and the forces of sanity, released from their long bondage, would ensure for the years to come a life of vigour and achievement and joy surpassing anything known in even the happiest eras of the past.

Christopher Logue

TO MY FELLOW ARTISTS

'The New Statesman', *March 22 1958*

1
Today, it came to me. How you
My friends who write, who draw
And carve, friends who make pictures,
Plays, finger delicate instruments,
Compose, or fake, or criticise, how
In the oncoming megaton bombardments,
All you stand for will be gone,
Like an arrow into hell.

2
It is strange, yet
If I tell you how sunlight glitters off
Intricate visions etched into breastplates
By Trojan silversmiths – you believe me,
You sanction my desires.

And if I say:
Around my bedposts birds have built their nests
That sing: No. No. – you share my anxiety,
My loss becomes your evidence.

And if I write:
When I flog salt, it rains; when I sell flour
It blows – you feel my hopelessness,
What's more, you understand my words.

But if I speak straight out and say:

Infatuated with cheap immortality,
Distinguished each from each by pains
You measure against pains, you stand
To lose the world and look alike as if
You spat each other out, you say:

Logue grinds his axe again. He's red –
Or cashing in. And you are right.
I have an axe to grind. Compared to you,
I'm red – and short of cash. So what?
I think, am weak, need help, have lived,
And will, with your permission, live.
Why should I puzzle you with words
When your beds are near sopping with blood?

And yet I puzzle you with words.

3
If – as many of you do – you base
All of your hope, all of that hope
Necessary to make a work of art,
On unborn generations, start
Hunting up a place to hide those works
You will contrive in privation.

Consider, my fellows, how all
The dead lovelies inside our museums,
Stones, books, things we have stolen,
Think how they will crumple up
One dusk between six and six-ten.
Spend your shilling. Sleep alone.

Especially you, Amis and Osborne,
Past masters at flogging your own
Contemptibility. Will you not champion
Your thoughts that were never contemptible?
And you, John Wain, you write letters
Defending your poetry. Will you not write
Against your certain destruction?

4
It is true.
They will say you are fools
Who know nothing of politics.
Women and artists must keep out of politics.

They will suggest –
Politely, politely – your hair
Is too long for sanity.
Even though you are bald with worry.

They will,
With their reason,
Prove your unreasonableness.
Though you are dying from rationality.

They will do all in their power,
And their power is great,
To shut you up, until

Recommending your wife's sexual niceties,
Or lamenting her
Loose in the hilts,

You thrive like milestones for whom,
The Queen's green pounds
Were contagious.

5
Listen, I beg you. Lately,
In a publication called *Sunday Times*
They spilled their fetid gifts of mind.

Saying:
You are confused about things, yes? But,
Recommending the death of the country
In the name of the country, we must bomb
If we must bomb. Bomb like King Billy,
For the English have something to die for.

They do not speak about something to live for.

Saying:
In the names of loyalty, faith, integrity,
How vile are those who want a life here,
Minus the current notions of democracy.

Not speaking of those who wish to die here.

The death before dishonour, boys.
The death before gestapo, boys.
The death before a tyrant, boys.
The death before the *Sunday Times*.

But where is the dishonour, gestapo,
Or tyrant? Who would want to dishonour
Or govern a cinder? My friends,
How difficult it is to speak
Out of anger to answer those who speak
Out of prejudice and complacency! Yet:

Those who imagine a horror
And commit a horror because of it,
Are called mad.

Those who talk desolation
And create desolation because of it,
Are called mad.

Thus the Ripper and Christie
Thought of whores.
Thus they think of our country.

6

So do you agree with them,
Spender, and Barker, and Auden?
And you, my newly married master, Eliot.
Will you adopt their lie by silence?
And having sold our flesh to war
Bequeath our bones to God . . . or,
Are there two sides to *this* question?

But I fear we are easily beaten.
So where shall we put them, our treasures?
Uncertain the disused chalk-pit.
Uncertain the bank's steel vaults.
And the holds of ships are uncertain.

We must beg permission
To hang our paintings underground.
Store books and stones in mines –
For the first time miners will see them.
But the rents will be high, underground.
I doubt if we can afford them.

Maybe they will let us
Into the deep bomb-lockers
Where the pilots and aimers sleep tight.
We must not be afraid to ask.
For the works of Angries
Will not scare the dedicated experts.

But we must remember to leave behind
Permanent signs. Signs that are
Easily read. Signs that say: So deep . . .
Under this many foot of stone . . .
Is the Film Institute, The Royal Court,
Better Books, the ICA.

Then can our six-handed grandsons –
Your unborn consolation –
Discover that we, too, had art.
And those who dare look
Over the jagged crater's rim
Will go down to the mauve bowl of London

And dig with their hands.
While their guards
Watch out for tyrants and food and sun.
Think, men of no future
But with a name to come.

Alex Comfort

THE PEOPLE MUST TAKE OVER

The Campaign for Nuclear Disarmament was born on February 17 1958 at a public meeting in the Central Hall, Westminster, which overflowed into no fewer than five other halls. One of the speakers was biologist, poet and novelist Alex Comfort. The People Must Take Over *is the text of his speech that night.*

On or about April 25, 1937, aircraft of the Axis powers bombed the Spanish city of Guernica, causing about 5,000 casualties.

That event, therefore took place only 20 years ago; it was received with horror and shame in almost every country of the world. It seemed to mark a fundamental change for the worse in thinking of our culture.

I suppose today we could call it the first example of a praiseworthy realism toward civilian casualties.

A few years later, about the time of the outbreak of the Second World War, physicists in several countries realised that nuclear energy could probably be released, and that it might provide a new and uniquely terrible military weapon.

Einstein, in America, because he knew what Fascist governments might do with such a weapon, finally decided to write the letter to Roosevelt which set afoot the Western atomic bomb project.

At the same time, the German physicists were equally aware what might happen if Hitler were to get hold of atomic weapons.

They risked their careers and their lives by dragging their feet. Hitler did not get the bomb.

It was the British and American scientists who trusted the undertakings given them by democratic governments, and who were rewarded by seeing atomic bombs dropped without warning on two civilian populations in an enemy country which was already attempting to treat for peace. People are still dying of that action today.

Within ten years of this first and wholly gratuitous use of atomic weapons, within 20 years of Guernica, all the governments of the major powers, Britain, the U.S.A. and Russia, and many of the official leaders of political parties in this country, are committed to the idea that civilian massacre, and the threat of it, are normal and proper means of defence.

Our government considers them proper means of defending what they value in our way of life.

They expect, in fact, to rely on the threat alone, but to maintain that threat they are making deliberate and serious preparation to reply to any military attack with hydrogen bombs, knowing, as they do know, that those bombs if fired will kill enough of the human race, born and unborn, inside enemy territories and outside them, to risk bringing human history to an end.

In pursuit of that policy, grave risks are being taken with the health of the world – risks which are at present incalculable, irreversible, and likely to exert their effects for generations to come.

Innocent people have already been killed and injured, in Japan, in the Marshall Islands, and elsewhere. More will be killed and injured by every Russian, American or British nuclear test which releases radio-activity.

Aircraft are flying about, over Great Britain, and elsewhere, which are admittedly carrying radio-active material. Any place which is accidentally contaminated by this material may be made uninhabitable for years.

There is no difference of scientific opinion about the reality of any of these risks – only about their extent. The governments of the nuclear powers, America, Russia and Britain, are apparently satisfied that the risks are justified by defence. The peoples of the world are not.

The official defence of this policy is that the threat is enough. It is to serve as a deterrent. It is, indeed, a deterrent – to those countries which would like to support us rather than the Russians: a deterrent to all constructive policy on our part. Whether it is a deterrent against war I doubt very much.

Common sense suggests that if it is wrong to behave like madmen, it is wrong to threaten to behave like madmen.

This meeting has been called tonight, I believe, far less to argue the case against nuclear weapons than to give expression to the growing volume of opinion which already rejects those weapons and the policy behind them.

I think that most of you who are here tonight, and in the other five halls which we have had to take, have come not to hear reasons for thinking the present policy insane, but to hear what action you personally can take to resist it before it destroys us all.

I have not come to talk about the biological effects of radiation. An American general recently said that 'current planning estimates' run in terms of hundreds of millions of casualties. That kind of statement seems to me to come within the field of mental derangement.

The present Western, and presumably Russian, policy of massive retaliation means meeting the threat of military, or even political defeat, not by dying to the last man, a gesture which may be unnecessary but is at least not contemptible, but by killing to the last child, and running the real and conscious risk of bringing human history to an end.

That I submit, is a policy for madmen, not statesmen; it is unworthy of normal human beings.

Now I believe that there are no circumstances in which the use of these weapons, defensively or offensively, could be justified or excused, whatever the alternative.

However great are the physical risks which we and our children run from the radio-active pollution of the air, they seem to me less than the mischief done to our own self-respect by the acceptance of these monstrous policies.

The threat on which we are depending for the defence of our values its itself eroding those values to a point at which they will not be worth defending, against Communism or anything else.

Walter Millis, the military historian, has written this, in the 'New York Times Magazine':

> 'Any society which pins its hopes of survival on its technical ability to massacre millions of the enemy's innocent noncombatants, which is at the same time reckless of its responsibility for poisoning in the name of self-defence, the atmosphere and food-bearing soil of the whole earth, has accepted a moral degradation which denies it any title to freedom within itself.'

That is the real objection, I believe, to these weapons. They do not differ only in degree from orthodox bombs. Between Guernica and Coventry and Hamburg on one hand, and Hiroshima on the other, we took the step from cruelty which is always present in war, into insanity.

If we are asked, as we will be, 'What is your alternative? How else do you think this country should be defended?' we may indeed propose alternative policies.

But we are bound, in any case, to reply: 'Whatever policy may be right, this one is wrong.' That it demands no more detailed alternative for us to reject it than did Hitler's gas chambers or Stalin's purges. It is a policy from the same stable. It is unworthy of sane human beings.

The moral responsibility for the action of the U.S.A. or the Soviet Union lies in those countries. The moral responsibility for the actions of Britain lies with us.

Unlike the leaders of all the major parties, I think that this is an occasion where the manifestly right course of action is also the wise and expedient course of action.

It has been suggested that if the public were to be asked directly whether Britain should renounce nuclear weapons, unilaterally and without further argument, they would not take the very real risks involved. I say, they are real risks, though not greater than those we are running today.

If it is left to the parties, that issue never will be presented to them in a direct and honest form. But I do know that if any government or party were to announce that repudiation, the whole moral atmosphere of this country would change overnight, and I do not think that change would remain purely domestic.

For many years now, and most evidently since last year, the salient new factor in the politics of Europe has been the growing discontent of ordinary men and women with the policies of inhumanity; of anger and disillusion with compromises, double talk and cruelty, and with the complete lack of principle which has become the rule in government since Hitler.

In Russia, and in the other Communist countries, reason has been genuinely in revolt: and scientists there have rebelled, and rebelled effectively, against the abuse of science, as the younger generation is rebelling against Stalinism. The atomic scientist Kapitza spent years under house arrest for refusing to work on atomic bombs.

In Germany, physicists have declared that they will not lend themselves to the development of nuclear weapons.

I choose scientists as examples, not because they have any greater moral duty to rebel against folly than others, but because in Britain and America they have been culpably slow to do so; among the public at large there is growing anger and apprehension all over Europe at the risks which are being run, and the absence of good faith among those who are running them.

However much this discontent is exploited for electoral purposes, I do not see the parties today giving an answer to the hundreds of people, of all persuasions, who are asking what they, individually, can do to reassert the rule of sanity.

That is the function of the campaign which we are launching here tonight: to make every individual reassume the moral responsibility for opposing public insanity. The issue is one for direct action by every one of us.

We are not at the mercy of the Government, nor of events, nor of the policy of other nations, nor of the world situation, if we are prepared as a public to be sufficiently combative.

I would remind you that once already in the last two years we have seen public opinion assert itself on a moral issue through the sheer force of unorganised indignation. The response which we have received from you tonight is of that same order.

Within the coming weeks we intend to raise throughout the country a solid body of opposition to the whole strategy of moral bankruptcy and ceremonial suicide which the hydrogen bomb epitomises, to all the mentally under-privileged double-talk by which it has been justified.

I would urge every one of us at this meeting to go home determined to become a living focus of that opposition. Some of us are going to march to Aldermaston on Good Friday, whether the Minister of Works likes it or not. Some of us live in areas which have been selected to receive American guided missile bases.

The Government is intensely anxious about public reaction to those bases, and is trying to keep their location secret.

If there are no local committees in your area, keeping their eyes open for base building activity, form one. If there is no focus for public opposition to nuclear tests and nuclear weapons in your district, in your church, among your neighbours, become one. If you are not already exerting pressure on your Member, on the Prime Minister, on the Press, on any scientists involved in unethical projects whose addresses you can get, begin to do so now, by letter and by lobbies.

It is high time we held some atomic tests of our own – in Downing Street.

Much has been said about a summit conference. Sanity is always hardest to restore at the summit – the air there is rarefied. It seems to affect the brain. We can reassert it at the base.

The people must take over – you must take over. The leaders of all the parties are waiting, as they always wait on any issue of principle, to follow public opinion. We can coerce them.

Gaitskell and Bevan say they will not abandon the H-bomb unilaterally. If they were here tonight, they would see that in this issue their party is abandoning them unilaterally.

We can make Britain offer the world something which is virtually forgotten – moral leadership. Let us make this country stand on the side of human decency and human sanity – alone if necessary. It has done so before. If it does so again I do not think we need fear the consequences.

Philip Toynbee

ANSWERS TO THOSE WHO OPPOSE NUCLEAR DISARMAMENT

Novelist and journalist Philip Toynbee was one of the first volunteer platform speakers for CND. *His background equipped him to talk about modern warfare. He held a commission in the Intelligence Corps, 1940-1942, in the Ministry of Economic Warfare, 1942-1944, and on the staff of the Supreme Headquarters, Allied Expeditionary Force, France and Belgium, 1944-1945.* Answers To Those Who Oppose Nuclear Disarmament *was written for* ' Peace News ', *March 21 1958.*

It is very important that those of us who support the immediate unilateral nuclear disarmament of the West should try to answer the specific points raised against us by our opponents.

It is all too easy to go on saying the same things to the converted without paying any attention to the unconverted.

Now the principal and most obvious point which is made against us is that even if the West does give a good example to the world by renouncing their own nuclear weapons, Russia will certainly not follow suit. Therefore, the only result of our action will be the domination, perhaps the occupation, of the whole world by Russian Communism.

We have every right to answer this, in the first place, by saying that we think this an improbable result. It does not seem that the Russians have greatly enjoyed their experience of trying to hold down Eastern Europe.

Is it likely that they'd try to repeat this experience in such indigestible countries as France, Sweden, Italy, Britain and America?

Even if there were little armed resistance to Russian occupation inside these countries, there would be at least a thousand million sullen opponents of the occupying forces throughout the occupied democratic world. Is this a prospect, after Hungary, which would seem attractive to Mr Khrushchev?

As I say, we can make this our first reply. But there are many answers to it, and if we stick to this line alone I believe we shall get ourselves bogged down in an infinite series of speculations and counter-speculations.

If we are to be honest we must admit that by advocating *Western* – and not merely British – renunciation, we are taking a very grave risk of handing over the world to Communism.

We should say that we are taking that risk with open eyes, believing it to be a far lesser risk that the risk which is taken by continuing the arms race.

We must say that we think it a lesser evil that the world should be dominated by Russia than that the world should be destroyed or mutilated by nuclear warfare.

The present historical situation is a typically tragic one in that we cannot choose between a certain good and a certain evil; we can only choose the lesser of two evils.

To my own way of thinking a Russian occupation of the West would be not only a terrible historical retrogression: it would also involve acute personal suffering to many brave and innocent people, and the exercise of power in a wicked way.

Nevertheless, I am in no doubt at all that it is both wise and right to choose to take that risk rather than to choose the continued and deadly risk of lacerating tens of millions by nuclear warfare. Even under Communism life goes on and life is capable of improvement.

In the last five years there have been great changes within the Communist world, and those changes are still continuing.

The lesson of Hungary is not that brave men and women can do nothing against tanks, but that brave men and women are ultimately undefeatable.

In fact, the post-Stalin epoch has done much to disprove the gloomy apocalyptics of George Orwell. If a regime is utterly against human nature it cannot survive *indefinitely*. It may survive for a tragically long time: it may even destroy the freedom and hope of a whole generation.

But it is surely very significant that even in Russia young people who have known nothing except a Communist regime are more and more crying out for the freedom and the tolerance which they have never known.

If I were to put it personally, and rather melodramatically, I'd say that I would much rather die after a Communist occupation of my country than before it. Rather than be uselessly atomised I would like to make whatever protest I could against the occupying forces and die with some small sense of a purpose achieved.

The more violent of our opponets accuse us of acting from motives of personal fear. Let me say here that I do not regard fear as a base emotion. To feel no fear in a fearful situation is to be sub-humanly stupid, not super-humanly brave. Everything depends on how we deal with our fear.

I will frankly admit that the present situation makes me afraid for my own skin. I don't want to die just yet. There are many, many things I should like to get done before my death.

But I hope and believe that I am at least as much afraid for my children and my friends, my country and my world, as I am for myself. We are made in such a way that we inevitably think first of our immediate circle and surroundings. I think of the destruction of Suffolk, London and Oxford far more vividly than I am able to think of the destruction of the Crimea, Omsk or Moscow.

But if, in a purely hypothetical situation, I could ensure the safety of this country by launching rockets on Russia I would not dream of doing so.

Our natural love for those who are dear to us must be imaginatively reinforced by a moral awareness of the millions who are remote from us. In fact, we should try to be afraid for the Russians as well as for ourselves – and this, as it happens, is made all the easier for us by the fact that in the present situation all our fates are tightly bound together.

I see nothing brave or heroic in a continuation of the arms race. The brave thing to do, surely, is to renounce these wicked weapons because they are wicked, *and to do so in the full knowledge of the risk that we are taking.*

If our policy is accepted and if the worst that is possible were to come from it we shall need all the courage we have to face the new situation with honour and usefulness.

Should the Russians occupy us and should they behave towards us as they have behaved in other occupied countries we would have, as individuals, to say no. Asked to betray a friend, or to write a lie, we will refuse.

If enough of us refused we would make it impossible for the occupiers to continue with that kind of policy.

But many, many people will be killed for their refusals. I would prefer to be one of those – and hope that I might have the courage to be one of them – rather than to be one of the millions of useless victims of nuclear warfare.

Sir Richard Acland

WAGING PEACE

Sir Richard Acland was one of the earliest political conscientious objectors against nuclear weapons, resigning a Labour seat in the House of Commons in 1955 as a protest against his party's decision to support the Conservative Government's intention to manufacture the hydrogen bomb. Waging Peace, *written for* 'Peace News', *September 26 1958, is a summary of his book of the same name.*

Britain is drifting to destruction and defeat. Destruction because no serious observer could put the odds about nuclear war in 1959 at anything better than fifty-to-one against. This corresponds fairly well with our feelings of relative immediate security. But fairly good chances that the nuclear war probably won't happen in 1959 or 1960 or 1961 create in the end an appallingly bad chance that it probably will happen some time in the coming century.

Defeat, because we now have to meet a challenge for which there is no precedent in history. It is directed against us not only at the military, but at the economic, political and social level at the same time. Far too many people talk and think and feel as if military weapons were the only things that we have to take into account as we try to fit ourselves to meet the Communist challenge.

If we were now engaged in military war against the Communists with the weapons and strategy of 1914-18, so that an entrenched battle line stretched from Baltic to Mediterranean, and if this line were being steadily driven back, say at an average rate of a hundred miles a year, we would be thinking of almost nothing else. All public attention would be focused on it. Every newspaper and every serious citizen would be anxiously discussing the prospects. But none of this happens when we are steadily falling back on the economic, social and political front. Hardly anyone even considers the ways in which we might do better.

If these dangers are to be met, Britain must have a policy adequate to them.

Abandonment of nuclear weapons is the first essential of such a policy.

This involves risk, but it is not possible to make a choice which does not involve risk. The policy of our leaders is as much a choice as any other policy. And it is the policy most likely to lead to death for our people and for their ideals.

The pre-war years should have warned us of this, for the lesson of the 1930's is just this: that our leaders by their timidity eventually brought us to almost certain destruction.

In 1939 they led us into a war which we were bound to lose. The fact that in the end it also chanced that we emerged with military victory does not affect the judgment. But it will be our stupidity, not theirs, if we allow them to do the same sort of thing all over again.

We must learn the lesson of the 'thirties, take our eyes off the next couple of years, look right down to the end of the course which we are pursuing now, and have the courage to see, unflinchingly, that it is leading us either to almost certain destruction in nuclear war, or to defeat in the cold war, or to both.

What are the implications of abandoning nuclear armaments? Morally, the plain Christian truth is perfectly clear: we ought to be ready to submit to all the worst that Atheist Communism can do to us rather than resist it by preparing to slaughter forty or fifty million Russian men, women and children. Nevertheless, men of good will in Britain fear failure to resist Communism would lead to the imposition of a totalitarian State to which there is no foreseeable end.

Communist tyranny could not last for ever. How and when it would end we do not know; but that it would end is certain. Something recognisably British would live through the whole persecution and come out at the end.

But in fact Russian occupation is not even likely. It would be contrary to the Russian leaders' own estimate of what is to their advantage.

They must know now that they cannot impose Communism by force, while on the other hand they stand to lose enormously in world opinion by trying to do so.

Consider Hungary. Is it right to suppose that the present rulers of Russia will have concluded from Hungary that Communism *can* be imposed on all the world by force? Surely this ignores the question of scale?

It has always been known to the Russians and to everyone else that any great nation with immense military strength can always crush a rebellion, however courageous, in a little country with no military power at all.

The great shocks to the Russians must have been the disproportionate amount of force that they had to use; the dogged courage of workers and intellectuals giving their lives to escape the Communist yoke; and the amount of ideological doubt that was spread among their own European troops, who actually had to be replaced by Asian units before the real job was done.

There were only a few million people in Hungary; there are well over a billion in the non-Communist world today. The most elementary arithmetic must surely persuade the Russian high command, not that they can, but they cannot impose Communism on the whole world by physical force.

We should remember Russia is vulnerable. As Lord Chandos has said: 'Is it possible to turn out one hundred and fifty thousand students on a five-year course from one Academy alone and then expect them at the end not to start thinking a little bit for themselves?'

So much for the risks we take in nuclear disarmament. Our present policy places our ideals in much more serious danger by failing to take the initiative in positive policies. Nuclear disengagement would be perhaps the much-needed first step in overcoming mistrust.

We have tried for years to negotiate disarmament, but is there any chance of taking the first steps unless something else has already begun to change the mood of the world? Certainly there is no short cut, it may take fifty years; but some bold step there must be.

Similarly, Britain's disengagement would enable her to play the part of initiator in aid to under-developed countries through international bodies, in building up an international police force, and in many other ways all of which are at present barred because any action Britain takes now is seen inevitably as that of America's junior H-bomb partner.

I do not recommend a policy of absolute pacifism because, in my opinion, there is not the slightest chance that the British electorate will vote for it and sustain it at any time in the twentieth century. By contrast, I think there is a fair chance that the British people will decide to give up all nuclear weapons and abandon any idea of ever again participating in world-scale war.

James Cameron

ONE IN FIVE MUST KNOW

One of Britain's most popular and most respected newspaper correspondents, James Cameron saw the Bikini H-bomb explosion and visited Hiroshima. His account of a Women's Voluntary Service One In Five *Civil Defence first published in 'Lilliput' and subsequently popularised as a pamphlet. The italicised quotations in the text are from 'Hiroshima' by John Hersey.*

Father Kleinsorge never knew how he got out of the house. The next things he was conscious of were that he was wandering around in his underwear, bleeding from cuts in his flank, and all the buildings about had fallen down ... that the day had turned dark, and that Murata-san, the housekeeper, was nearby, crying over and over: 'Shu Jesu, awaremi tamai! – Oh Jesus, have pity!'

The ladies of the Women's Voluntary Service sit around the long table in their headquarters, their Staff College for Civil Defence, here in the year 1960, good and decent people with good and decent values, as befits gentlefolk confronted with a challenge both cosmic and disagreeable.

'We pull no punches,' said the head lady, 'we shall take as our example the biggest bomb yet invented, and see what this will mean in our own homes. Certainly there will be risks ....'

All around the heads nod gratefully, relieved to have the dilemma of life and death clarified in a moment of revelation, and with taste. This is a briefing for the One in Five Scheme 'to inform one in every five women of the country what she has to do to protect her home and family in a nuclear war.' One in five. The voice of the lady in the green uniform is assured, confident, conciliatory, tranquil, U, practised, with a special note of democratic good humour far removed from irony. One in five must know.

'What we're against, of course, is the note of defeatism – that people, you know, think it's not *worth* bringing up a family, that almost anything is better than being destroyed. Well, that is the worst thing that can happen to a nation, isn't it? We have talked to girls in the Bank of England, the I.C.I., the Port of London Authority, the big stores, the big distilleries – everywhere; we've even talked to them in the launderette. (Laughter.) Don't think we haven't had opposition; we've been attacked in the cruellest way: ridicule. Most by those Nuclear Disarmament people; they don't want *us* to have the bomb, and we detract from that sort of plan. But we are standing firm, aren't we? We know, don't we, that the great thing is to understand how to *minimise* it . . . . ?'

. . . of a hundred and fifty doctors in the city, sixty-five were already dead and most of the rest were wounded. Of 1,780 nurses, 1,654 were dead or too badly hurt to work. In the biggest hospital only six doctors out of thirty were able to function, and only ten nurses out of more than two hundred . . . In a city of 254,000 nearly 100,000 had been killed or doomed at one blow. 100,000 more were hurt. At least 10,000 made their way to the hospital.

. . . The people in the suffocating crowd wept and cried for Dr. Sasaki to hear: ' Sensei! Doctor! . . . Tugged here and there in his stockinged feet, bewildered by the numbers, staggered by so much raw flesh, Dr. Sasaki lost all sense of profession and stopped working as a skilful surgeon and a sympathetic man; he became an automaton, mechanically wiping, daubing, winding, wiping, daubing, winding . . . .

' You see,' says the tall trim lady, tapping her pencil against her notes, ' in our first talk we sort of cover the *explosion*, and the things we can do to mitigate it in our own homes. We must cater for the *biggest* bombs, too. We reckon on getting three warnings, after all. First of all we hope we'll get a warning of a *war*, in the first place – like 1939, you remember; they said there'd be one. Some of us might think of getting ready then. Then we hope there'll be a warning of the missiles coming, though I'm afraid we can't promise too much. There is, however, a third warning: the bomb itself gives its *own* warning by exploding, unless, of course, you're underneath it, by giving off a very bright light.

' Now the bomb produces three dangers: heat, blast, and radioactivity. The fireball when the bomb explodes is very hot indeed, but it lasts only about twenty seconds, you know. Our first thought should be, how to keep it out of our houses. This is the bit where we get misquoted and ridiculed, because this is where you have to whitewash your windows. I know, but it does deflect eighty per cent of the heat. Try not to have anything frilly in the path of where the heat may come. When you see that bright light, that is the bomb, then what you ought to do is get into the shadow. Do have a bucket of water, and have your bath filled, and do soak your soft furnishings in a solution of borax and water – it does work, you know; flame-proof. If you are caught outside, just you *turn your back to it . . .*'

. . . They did not move and he realised they were too weak to lift themselves. He reached down and took a woman by the hands, but her skin slipped off in huge glove-like pieces . . . He had to keep consciously repeating to himself: ' These are human beings . . .'

' I do really suggest that you take a short course in home nursing,' says the lady, ' because it is awfully useful in such circumstances. The next danger is Blast. The experts say it might have a slightly different action than in the last war – more like a tornado or a typhoon, really. Maybe you can't do awfully much about saving the house. But the blast doesn't come until a minute and a half after the explosion. And you'll remember you had twenty seconds warning of the heat – so actually you've got a bit of time. Now: you're in your bit of shadow, aren't you, as we said. Now you find a nice dip in the ground to lie in. You may get cuts from bits of glass and things, so just whip out a sterile dressing and put it on. And, of course, treat for shock . . .'

. . . The hurt ones were quiet; no one wept, much less screamed in pain; no one complained; none of the many who died did so noisily; very few people even spoke. And when Father Kleinsorge gave water to some whose faces had been blotted out by flash burns, they took their share and then raised themselves a little and bowed to him, in thanks . . .

' There is of course that third danger, I was saying, because when the fireball comes it sort of sucks up all the stuff, dust and things, into a mushroom-shaped cloud; I'm sure you've seen the pictures. Well . . . Well of course that's over the central devastation area, and we're not really interested in that, are we, since we can't do very much there; I mean everyone's dead in a way. What we're interested in is that *residual* radioactivity blowing all about; you see you may be in a fall-out area in due course. They say the cloud is apt to travel at about twenty miles an hour, and what *that* means is that if you are twenty miles away, and done your preparations, and so on, you've got about an hour to get yourself all ready. So we advise you to prepare what we call our " Refuge Room " – that is to say, the place in your house that's *central;* you know, plenty of walls and ceilings. If I were you I'd thicken my walls with earth. There's likely to be a lot of dust giving off gamma-rays and stuff, and you really want to get as far away from that as you can, actually. The thing about radioactive material is just that you have to let it all *decay* – you know, there's not much else you can do with it; you can't *burn* gamma rays or anything. However, it doesn't affect inanimate things, you know, only living tissues. The point to remember is it gives you radiation sickness if you get that sort of dust on you. One good thing about it you ought to know is, it isn't infectious. Nor contagious. You can't *catch* radiation sickness, except if the fall-out drops on you; what I mean is you can't get it from a friend . . . .'

. . . and they were all in the same nightmarish state: their faces were wholly burned, their eye sockets were hollow, the fluid from their melted eyes had run down their cheeks. (They must have had their faces upturned when the bomb went off; perhaps they were anti-aircraft personnel.) Their mouths were mere swollen, pus-covered wounds, which they could not bear to stretch enough to admit the spout of a teapot . . .

'Also of course you must remember there are different *sizes* of bombs. They wouldn't use a big bomb on a small area, would they? Still – London, so to speak, would be worth quite a big one. Of course, you know, some people *do* get alarmed when you tell them about this sort of thing. But I can tell you this: I've never left any room yet without *someone* saying how she'd been reassured.'

'Think twice before you give this man blood transfusion; with atom-bomb patients we are not at all sure that, if you stick needles into them, they will ever stop bleeding . . .' (Hospital notice from 'Hiroshima.'*)*

'Then there's the question of how you're going to support yourself in the refuge room, because you may be there some time. We must obey orders. We must do what we're *told*. I mean, we must stay in the refuge-room until someone comes and tells us to get out. I can't tell you how long; maybe many days, because of the dust. One of our leaflets has the complete list of things to stock up with – food, you know, and water, and medicines. *Do* take that home nursing course. Then again, we're going to be in each other's company, *very* close indeed – well, we must be normal, and cheerful; take one or two books you've always wanted to read and never had the time . . .'

. . . she began to shiver heavily, and again said it was cold. Father Kleinsorge borrowed a blanket from someone nearby and wrapped her up, but she shook more and more, and said again 'I am so cold,' and then she suddenly stopped shivering, and was dead.

Then there was tea.

'I imagine everyone must admire your efforts, but isn't there a rather curious political effect in being so – well cosy?'

'I assure you we have no politics.'

'Can anyone have any public activity without being in some way political?'

'We don't have any politics at all. We are very loyal.'

'I know, but – this idea of a Do-It-Yourself Survival Kit. Do you yourselves believe in it?'

'I have actually heard,' said a lady, 'that there are some of those Disarmament people who say they would sooner have the Russians here than have the bomb go off; what an awful thing; you see what we have to fight.'

...and then the flames came along the street and entered his house. In a paroxysm of terrified strength he freed himself and ran down the alleys of Noboricho, hemmed in by the fires he had said would never come. He began at once to behave like an old man; two months later his hair was white.

'The point is – I wonder, did you ever see Hiroshima?'

'No.'

'I did.'

Bertrand Russell

PLANETARY EFFULGENCE

'The New Statesman', *September 5, 1959*

Science in Mars had been making extraordinarily rapid progress. The territory of Mars was divided between two great empires, the Alphas and the Betas, and it was their competition, more than any other one cause, which had led to the immense development of technique. In this competition neither side secured any advantage over the other. This fact caused universal disquiet, since each side felt that only its own supremacy could secure the future of life. Among the more thoughtful Martians, a feeling developed that security required the conquest of other planets.

At last there came a day when the Alphas and the Betas, alike, found themselves able to dispatch projectiles to Earth containing Martian scientists provided with means of survival in a strange environment. Each side simultaneously dispatched projectiles, which duly reached their terrestrial target. One of them fell in what the inhabitants of Earth called 'The United States', and the other in what they called 'Russia'. To the great disappointment of the scientists, they were a little too late for many of the investigations which they had hoped to make. They found large cities, partially destroyed; vast machines, some of them still in operation; storehouses of food; and large ships tossing aimlessly on stormy seas. Wherever they found such things, they also found human bodies, but all the bodies were lifeless.

The Martian scientists, by means of their super-radar, had discovered that on Earth, as in Mars, power was divided between two factions which, on Earth, were called the As and the Bs. It had been hoped that intercourse with the curious beings inhabiting Earth might add to Martian wisdom. But, unfortunately, life on Earth had become extinct a few months before the arrival of the projectiles.

At first the scientific disappointment was keen; but before very long cryptologists, linguists and historians succeeded in deciphering the immense mass of records accumulated by these odd beings while they still lived. The Alphas and the Betas from Mars each drew up very full reports on what they had discovered about Tellurian thought and history. There was very little difference between the two reports. So long as each of the two factions remain unidentified, what A said about itself and about B was indistinguishable from what B said about itself and about A. It appeared that, according to each side, the other side wanted world dominion and wished all power to be in the hands of heartless officials whom the one side designated as bureaucrats and the other as capitalists.

Each side held that the other advocated a soulless mechanism which should grind out engines of war without any regard to human happiness. Each side believed that the other, by unscrupulous machinations, was endeavouring to promote world war in spite of the obvious danger to all. Each side declared loudly: 'We, who stand for peace and justice and truth, dare not relax our vigilance or cease to increase our armaments, because the other side is so wicked.' The two Martian reports, drawn up by the Alphas and the Betas respectively, had similarities exactly like those of the As and Bs whom they were describing. Each ended up with a moral to its government. The moral was this: 'These foolish inhabitants of Earth forgot the obvious lesson that their situation should have taught them, namely, that it is necessary to be stronger than the other side. We hope that the government to which we are reporting will learn this salutary lesson from the awful warning of the catastrophe of our sister planet.'

The governments of the Alphas and the Betas, alike, listened to the reports of their Tellurian experts and, alike, determined that their faction should be the stronger. A few years after this policy had been adopted by both the Alphas and the Betas, two projectiles reached Mars from Jupiter. Jupiter was divided between the Alephs and the Beths, and each had sent its own projectile. Like the Martian travellers to Earth, the Jovian travellers found life in Mars extinct, but they soon discovered the two reports which had been brought from Earth. They presented them to their respective governments, both of which accepted the Martian moral with which the two Martian reports had ended.

But as the Rulers of the two rival States of Alephs and Beths were finishing the drawing up of their comments, each had a strange, disquieting experience. A moving finger appeared, seized the pen from their astonished hand, and, without their co-operation, wrote these words: 'I am sorry I was so half-hearted at the time of Noah. (Signed) Cosmic President.' These words were deleted by the censor on each side and their strange occurrence was kept a profound secret.

Marghanita Laski

THE CIVIL DEFENCE WORKER'S STORY

These two short stories, The Civil Defence Worker's Story *by Marghanita Laski, and* Mrs MacNaughton's Story *by Naomi Mitchison, were written for a* CND *pamphlet,* Survivors: Fiction Based on Fact, *edited by Dr Antoinette Pirie. Each story describes in fictional terms a nuclear attack, but the factual basis is underlined by the references to official defence and civil defence publications.*

I joined the Civil Defence because it seemed, for a woman like me, the right thing to do. I was in Civil Defence in Hitler's War and I remembered how, before that one started, all the longhairs were saying there was no defence against the bomb, just like they were saying in the 1950's. Of course I knew that nuclear weapons were worse. It still seemed to me that as a trained switchboard operator (as I'd learned to be then), I'd a useful contribution to make to the defence of my country and to help those who were determined that our country should be able to survive a nuclear attack. So I got trained and volunteered for the daytime shift in any emergency – the evening didn't seem quite fair to my husband. I went to the post while the children were at school, and then at teatime Caroline, my youngest, would come by and pick me up on her way home.

It was about teatime when it happened. We didn't get any warning. We knew, of course, that the situation was tense. It was three days since we'd been told to have a full shift on duty, day and night, and down in the post – which was the cellar of a large old warehouse – besides myself there was Tom who was the boss, Steve and Gerald who both had advanced first-aid training and Maureen, our runner, who was just eighteen.

I believe the warning may have been about to come through when it happened. There was a call and I was putting out my hand to take it, and then there was the – I don't know what word to use – noise won't do, nor explosion nor any word we know. Remember we were 20 feet underground and nearly fourteen miles north east of London – central London, I mean, where we suppose it – or they – dropped They said we'd have to be prepared for a ten-megaton bomb on London. Nobody, nothing could prepare you for what we heard and even now we don't know what kind of bomb it was or how many.

Because, of course, it wasn't only London. And it didn't happen only once.

I tried to call up headquarters. I can't tell you how long after because I don't know. But I tried to call up headquarters and it was all dead. It shouldn't have been but it was. Tom said the earth-tremors must have done something they hadn't expected. We tried the battery radio; there was a voice, not like a human voice at all, saying 'O God, O God, O God,' on and on and on. After a while we couldn't stand it. We couldn't get anyone else. Gerald said, 'We're on our own for the moment it seems.' But we knew what to do. This was what we'd been trained for. I had to stand by the telephone to receive and send out information. The others had to go up and help as soon as they could and plot damage and fallout.[1] It was reckoned it would be safe for them to go up for short periods when the radiation rate registered on the meters was less than 10r per hour.[2]

The first time they started to try to go up, it was no good. It was too hot. You could tell that, they said, as soon as they opened the first door. From the dose rate it looked as if we must be in Zone Z.[3]

I think it must have been for about three days that they kept on trying, and each time stopped by the radiation. We ate and we dozed – you couldn't call it sleeping – and every hour I tried the telephone and the radio. When in the end they did go up, I went with them. I told you it happened about teatime.

According to the meters the radiation level was about 10r per hour. That was what we'd been told to expect and for short periods, we could take this.

It should have been noon when we went up but it was dark, thick dark, full of dust and smoke.[4] Our post was on the outskirts of the town, by a filling station, a row of shops, some streets of new houses. You could see through the dust that there were flames here and there and sometimes a red glow. You couldn't walk properly. There were fallen bricks, and beams and bits of metal. Once I got my feet caught in what must have been a pram.

I was looking at the ground, trying to see where to put my feet, and I saw the body of a child. It was burnt all over, no flesh, no means of seeing whether it was a boy or a girl. It was the right size for Caroline. We went on, groping after each other in the dust.

Soon we went down again. There was nothing we could do then. We should have mapped fallout and damage, collected the wounded, perhaps set up a field kitchen, dressed simple wounds on the spot. But as far as we dared go from the shelter we saw no one but the burnt child. If we went further than those few yards we wouldn't find our way back again.[4] We went down for the rest of that day and night.

Next day the rain was falling. If you paused to think what was in that rain – but we couldn't pause to think. Everything we could see seemed to be burnt, shops, filling-stations, houses. They'd said there might be fire, but not so far out, not like this. It must have caught everything that could burn, wood, paint, petrol, curtains, people.

Someone was crawling over the debris. He made queer soft movements with his arms towards us. I don't know if he was speaking and I couldn't hear through my helmet, or if he had no voice. We saw, behind him, there'd been a garden and in it one of the Anderson shelters left over from Hitler's war mostly sunk below ground and with earth on top.[5] Steve and Gerald went in. They brought out a woman. She was covered with vomit and her clothes were nearly burned off. Tom went in after them and brought out a boy. He was about six. He'd been vomiting too but was now dead.

We took the man and woman back to the post. What we should have done was to load them into ambulances – many should have come by now – sent them off to the nearest hospital, but all this was meaningless now. Anyway no one could get through till the roads were cleared. There wasn't much we could do for this couple. They were scorched rather than burnt but they'd had too much radiation.

We left Maureen down with them. I think she'd been mad for some days, trembling and moaning. It was no use any longer pretending she wasn't.

By the end of the week we had forty-seven people in the post. It was the best shelter we could give them. The radiation had dropped to 3r per hour. We knew we were shortening our lives, but what else could we do. The population of our town had been 58,000. We had forty-seven people alive and twelve of them died within the next week, ugly, painful deaths. There was one old man whose flesh slid off him as we carried him down, but he lived for four days afterwards. When we could, we tried to clear up on top. Thank God most of the bodies had been burned in the houses and those we found we threw on to the still smouldering heaps. The smell of the bodies, both those we burned and those we couldn't extricate, was unspeakable,[6] and there were more and more flies. Tom said that the birds must all have been killed or died. It's true, we never saw one, all that time.

After another week we wouldn't have been able to feed even our few survivors, but before it was over the helicopter managed to land. It had tried the day before, but there hadn't been enough clear space. So we cleared what used to be the garage forecourt and it came down.

There was an army officer in it besides the pilot. He said we must leave our wounded and come away. The only way to evacuate them would be by helicopter and it would be too slow. After all, we were only one of many posts in the London perimeter, and everywhere the conditions were like ours. No train could get through, no car, no aeroplane could land near enough to be any use. About forty miles to the north-west, he said, round Bedford there was a space of about 400 square miles where people were only mildly sick. There, he said, we could be of some use, as trained personnel, whereas our own wounded were bound to die anyway. I think this was true. He gave us some stuff to kill them with before we went. We left Maureen behind too.

In Bedford the houses were standing and the people were alive. They'd even managed to bring in some injured, but there were mostly from the countryside. There were a good many refugees like us from London and from East Anglia near the bases. None of us was able-bodied any more. Those who weren't sick from radiation were sick from fatigue and I think most of us were a little mad. Steve started walking back as soon as we got there. He said he'd forgotten to bring his wife.

Originally the idea had been to move the people in the Bedford area to Wales. They were taking the ones from the south-east to Devon and Cornwall and those from the middle of Yorkshire up to Scotland. But several things happened to prevent this. First, the planes came back with rumours that the people in the reception areas wouldn't take any more of ours. There wasn't the food, they said, and they were terrified of the radiation they said our people might bring with them. There was no possibility of this – it was just one of those wild panic rumours. At the end of six weeks I suppose most of the refugees and about a third of the people in our district had died or were obviously dying of burns, wounds, infections or radiation sickness. Then the petrol gave out, and soon after the electricity, because there was no more fuel.

We kept saying that help must come – but who was there to give it to us? America? The few terrible reports that came over the radio didn't let us suppose that any help could come from there. Russia? There was no help anywhere.

But, you know, even in the last ditch you can't help hoping. Sometimes, when we talked – we didn't much – we'd say that in the west, in Wales and Scotland and Cornwall, they'd build up a Britain once more. But now, a year after it happened, we've been forced to give up that hope. A plane came through a week ago bringing more medical supplies, though we'd more supplies than patients now; we'd have had more use for guns, if we were to manage to ration the last of the food. Anyway, the pilot said that the land in the west was too contaminated for safe crops.[7] The fallout had been building up over the year and the rain was bringing it down. He said they had to ration the food there too. They were trying to give the safe food from the deep-stores to the children and the young people and to make the older ones eat what they grew. And not many babies were being born, he said, and often they were born too soon and dead.[8]

We here shall all be dead before another year is over. I suppose you could say we died for our country. But we never meant our country to die too.

1. Civil Defence Instructors Notes. Warden Section. W.18, p.6. and W.19, C12.
2. Civil Defence Pocket Book No. 3. General Information p.21, Civil Defence Instructors Notes. Warden Section W36: p.2, 3.
3. Manual of Civil Defence Vol. 1 pamphlet No. 2 H.M.S.O. 1956 p.16.
4. Civil Defence Instructors Notes. Warden Section W20 p.3 para 20.
5. Manual of Civil Defence Vol. 1 pamphlet No. 1 p.52-53.
6. Civil Defence Instructors Notes. Warden Section W19 C7 para 4b.
7. After the attack described in 'The Biological and Environmental Effects of Nuclear War' (U.S. Govt. 1959) it was estimated that the N. Hemisphere would have averaged 1,000 millcuries per sq. mile of Strontium 90 and that heavily contaminated areas would have reached 300,000 mc/sq. mile of Strontium 90. This is too heavy for safe cultivation.
8. Hazards to man of nuclear and allied radiations. H.M.S.O. 1960 p.13. 'Biological and Environmental Effects of Nuclear War.' U.S. Govt. 1959 p.610.

Naomi Mitchison

MRS MacNAUGHTON'S STORY

My name is Fiona MacNaughton. I was on the District Council, and on this and that committee. I had my farm a little way out from Oban; sometimes in summer I used to let to a few boarders. They were all terribly taken with my garden. I could laugh about that if there was any laughter left in me. But there is not.

I had my little grand-daughter Nessie staying with me, Rob and Mary's youngest; it is only because of her that it is at all worth my while to be alive and sometimes, looking at her, I wonder. For I ask myself has she really escaped? Although she looks better than most of the other children, poor wee mites.

It was a light west wind and I was out in my garden, looking into the wind, so that I never saw the flash; I only – somehow – knew that something had happened. I turned and I saw the cloud go up. Then another. I thought about Rob and Mary; well I will not speak of that now, nor of much else. My other son was in the midlands of England: himself and – all of them. I had friends; it is all past.

Even knowing, I tried to telephone. But there was nothing, nothing. Then I began to think. There was the Civil Defence centre at Connel by the loch and I had said I would go over and help if there was ever any need. There was a stock of medicines, blankets and all that.

I gave the wee one a book and some sweeties and a great petting, saying I'd be gone for a while. It was on into evening before the first of the buses got through and then the rest, and I looking for my own ones. Just in case. It was not until a week or two after, when they began to die, that I could bring myself to be glad that Rob and Mary and Andy and Jean had not been among them; that it was all over for them almost before I had seen the cloud. The only train that got through had been standing at Garelochhead; the driver was burnt, but he carried on, the decent man; I remember he did not die for quite a while. He lifted a load all up from there to Arrochar; the woods were all on fire round him; it was the ones who had been working in their gardens, who had the burns. No train from further down Loch Long had a chance. The ones who came on the buses were from Alexandria, Balloch, the western edge of Dumbarton even. There were a few from Helensburgh who got across to the Lomond side road, but they had been badly caught by the Holy Loch bomb. They had the most terrible things to tell us; some of them had these burns that did not heal. The blankets were mostly used to bury them in. That is, until we began to see that there would be no more blankets and we could not afford to let the dead have any of them.

That first night the wind blew itself out and there was a calm. But, even while it seemed to be blowing, there must have been a current away above us that was bringing some of the evil stuff.[1] I have some sense and I kept Nessie in the house, but myself, I was working with the refugees. I started by bringing all my milk over to the centre; I thought it was the best way I could help. One of the doctors – he is dead now, but he was a fine young man – said to me that it was as good as poison. 'Throw it away!' he said, and he told me, quick, while he was dressing a burn (we still had dressings in those days) that the milk would be full of radioactive iodine and must on no account be given to anyone, above all not a child; it would damage the child's thyroid gland and give it a cancer or turn it into an idiot.[2]

We all know that now. Too well do we know it. But then it was news; he said to me: 'Go round to your neighbours, Mrs MacNaughton, and warn them all, above all those with bairns.' 'And mind, not a drop to Nessie.' So I did just that, but half of them laughed at me; it seemed against nature that good milk with nothing at all wrong in the look of it, could hurt a child. So it came about that I saw my nearest neighbour's three turning within months from lively bright children into listless miseries. One of them has just died; we all know that is best.

Yet at the time it seemed just crazy; Nessie was with me just because she'd had the measles and was needing good food. I did not think to do this extra washing of the vegetables till later.[3] And even so it had me puzzled, for we get our water from the high loch and it would get as much fall-out as the grass. I had not thought it out; when I did I began drawing water out of the old well that is fed by a spring from far underground. I look and look at Nessie and wonder, did I keep enough of the stuff away from her? Or will she have something secretly eating at her?

It is difficult now to remember just when things happened. The electricity went on for quite a while, since most of the hydro-electric stations were far enough from the towns. But there is no way of getting repairs. Some of the men have gone in for short times and tried to get what supplies and spares they could carry away in barrows, but it is terribly risky, even with rubber boots and gloves.

Of course there was no petrol after the first week, even with the hard rationing. I am wondering how long my poor old pony will last; he had to eat the grass, it must have been thick with fall-out.

For that matter even if the wind had not changed, the stuff would have come back to us, right round the world. As it has come to everyone everywhere. I gave the first milk to the calves and they are not looking too grand. The milk should be safe now with the radioactive iodine worn off [4] and I could wish I had more of it, but the cows are just not in calf, and there seems to be nothing one can do. It is the same for most of my neighbours' beasts.[5]

That's bad, for we have to do with our own food, what we can grow ourselves. The tins are all done. And I am terribly doubtful about the fish; the way it seems to be, the plankton that the herring feed on gets hold, some way, of the radioactive stuff in the water and it stands to reason the herring will be full of it. I try to get the bottom fish for Nessie, but even the nets and lines are wearing out. We were so used to getting things from elsewhere.

Maybe this worrying all the time about what we shall have to eat and to to wear is some help against the feeling, night and day, that we are cut off: utterly cut off. Long ago I broke up my radio; the case burnt well. Nessie found an old newspaper at the bottom of the press and wondered what it was. I can remember that it used to be said by both the Americans and the Russians that they could stand an atomic war because it would only kill one in three or maybe it was one in four of their populations; I do not care one bit if there are no Americans left or no Russians. I would not lift one finger to help either of them, if I saw one in trouble. And once I was a good Church member with a great belief in human brotherhood. It is as though love had been killed in me.

At first we tried to go on with the District Council and such. But it is too difficult, we had too much else to do, all of us, and it is no joke walking in to Oban, where I used to drive my wee van. The County Council was finished; it could not meet. We could still telephone, up to January, when the lines went down in a storm and could not be repaired, as far as Lochgilphead, so we know what our fellow members suffered. Dunoon was wiped out, the Education Office, the County Clerk's Office, the clerkesses that used to be so cheery, answering the 'phone. Even in Lochgilphead, there were some people burned and a terrible lot of sickness later. The hospital at Lochgilphead was to receive casualties from Glasgow; some got through but most were scared of heading south again; it was too near Holy Loch. I don't know how they got on later. Nobody has been that far for months. The County Engineer, that we used to see at the Oban meetings, tried to get through to Dunoon. He was a brave man but it's just not enough to be brave.

But anyway the County Council depends on grants from the Central Government. And there is no Government. There is no

A CND rally in Trafalgar Square

centre. Schools only go on because we, the parents and grandparents, pay the teachers in eggs or potatoes, peats or meal. Public Health is gradually breaking down, for want of equipment.

I am lucky that my hens are still laying. Nearer Glasgow, most of the poultry as well as the cattle have died; they say there is hardly a cattle beast left in Dalmally and Tyndrum, as well as Strachur way, even down in Kintyre. But when the haze came over the sky and the glow like hell-mouth at sunset[6] – and, some way, I had expected this – I kept in all the beasts from the in-by land and the hens, just as I kept in Nessie. I mind now, I smacked her for running out and my heart bleeds for it, but I know I was right. But, the way I was placed, I could not get the sheep from the high ground – indeed we had nowhere to put them under cover, none of us – and things have gone badly there. I would find a dead sheep here or there and when it came to lambing there were dead lambs and sick ewes.[7]

I did the best I could. It was clear to all of us that we'd need to go back to the old ways for harvesting. A few of us had a bit of diesel oil laid by for the tractors and some used it for harvesting, making out that something would happen one day, some help come. I slept with the key of the padlock under my pillow and I let it be known that I had a gun. Though there was a time one could leave one's house door unlocked and no thought of harm. We got together and cut the oats with scythes and bound by hand. I tried to wear gloves at first, but they hinder one and we had to be quick; now I am worried about the skin on my right hand. Not that there is anything to be done about it. You cannot buy so much as an aspirin in Oban. I get sore places on my insteps too, and my face, and my hair has fallen out in patches. There was a time I would have minded about that.[8]

What we could not harvest at the back-end was fed to the beasts. Again we needed to thresh by hand, since there was no fuel for the big threshers. But it is easy enough to make a flail though hard and slow work using one. But we were aware by now, that there would be no flour coming in and we must depend on our own oat meal. It is queer to think how little one used to value a loaf of bread!

We dug the potatoes with graips, as we could not use the tractor-spinners, all getting together as in the old days. Not one wee potato did we miss! One had a good feeling that they, at least, would be safe, though now I am not so sure, for the evil stuff works down into the soil.

We notice, too, that there are far too many grubs and caterpillars and such, and not the birds that used to clear them off for us. For the poor birds that flew about in the air while it was at its worst, dropped and died; it was sad, that. One is glad to see a sparrow, even.[9]

I do not know how long we can go on. For this first year we still had some stores; I even make a Christmas cake for Nessie and a few other wee ones. But nothing comes in. Will it, ever? And our health is going down. And we do not know what will happen to the children. It is too soon to tell. Perhaps when we do know, it will seem to us that we were still happy when we did not know.

1. Manual of Civil Defence vol. 1, pamphlet No. 1, p.40-41.
2. Biological and Environmental Effects of Nuclear War. U.S. Govt. 1959.
3. Manual of Civil Defence vol. 1, pamphlet No. 1, p.57.
4. The Radio Activity of Iodine is half decayed in 8 days.
5. Home Defence and the Farmer, p.27; and The Hazards to Man of Nuclear and Allied Radiations, p.13, para. 48.
6. Biological and Environmental Effects of Nuclear War. U.S. Govt. p.839.
7. Home Defence and the Farmer, p.9.
8. Manual of Civil Defence vol. 1, pamphlet No. 1, p.13.
9. Biological and Environmental Effects of Nuclear War. U.S. Govt. p.791.

Jacquetta Hawkes

NOW AT LAST

'The New Statesman', *July 5, 1958*

It is said that there were Amazons, but more likely
They were a myth.
Women have not gone to war; ours has been an agelong army
Of fluttering hands and retreating into the house
With eyes wet or very dry.
Afterwards the messenger or the telegram or just waiting and waiting.
But since Anno Domini 1945 it has been different. Quite different.
Men may still march away, yet the battlefield is everywhere,
It is the whole globe.
Now the sudden wings of death shadow more of earth
Than does the cone of night.
And the wings of death shadow more than time present,
They stretch out over time future casting their darkness
Over generation after generation.

Now at least we women must rouse ourselves to resistance
For this is our business. Indeed it is our business.
If once to live privately was a virtue, it is so no more;
If once pliability was a virtue, it is so no more;
If once blind loyalty was a virtue, it has ceased to be so;
If quietness and acceptance were virtues they can no longer be praised.
For now at last we have to resist
Not in battalions or in swaying crowds
But by one and one and one to the number of half the world.

A few men seem possessed by a devil
Begotten, perhaps, by hate out of a child's fear.
Others again have so imprisoned themselves with arguments, with pleasing sophistries
That they cannot see daylight;
And some have a stomach for sacrifice
Corrupted by a secret appetite for death.

But many more – and alas we women cannot blind ourselves to this obscenity –
Many more have remained as boys, just boys
Heedlessly playing. But the spring of the toys they are winding
Is death.
We must take power from these madmen, these prisoners, these perilous children.

Women have seldom been the great creators
Rather we have been the continuers, the protectors, the lovers of life.
Now life itself is threatened,
The breath of all creation happy under the sun.
So let us arm ourselves with the names of women
Who have been great in the cause of life.
With the names of Helen Keller and Marie Curie
Of Elizabeth Fry who died long ago, and Margery her kinswoman
Who died just too soon to be here tonight.
And with the name, surely to be honoured, of that young Helen Smit
Who forsook physics for the law when she found the devil
Her new director of studies.
With the names of Octavia Hill, Florence Nightingale, and Eleanor Rathbone.
Of Ellen Wilkinson and Eleanor Roosevelt,
Of Ulanova, even, who can scotch enmity beneath her toe.
And when we have armed ourselves with these names,
And with the knowledge of all those, nameless,
Who have lived to protect the weak, relieve suffering, misery and injustice,
Let us make it known with the wisdom of simplicity
And the strength of half the world
That war is no longer heroic or honourable
But murder, just plain murder. Cowardly. Base. Universal.
Let us make it known that we here in our island
Will have no more of it; will renounce the instruments of hate.
Love is still a virtue. Our greatest virtue.
But it must be for all men born of women –
For all mankind.

Donald Soper

THE ROAD TO ALDERMASTON

The Rev. Dr. Donald Soper, Methodist controversialist, had organised an abortive anti-H-bomb campaign long before CND *took the field. In* The Road to Aldermaston, *published in* 'Tribune' *on April 4 1958, he appealed for support for the first Aldermaston March.*

As I think of the Aldermaston march, I am reminded of the paradox that there is nothing so contemporary as the past.

One of the first bits of human writing scratched on a stone dug out of the sands of the Middle East reads: 'What a world we live in, children no longer obey their parents and everybody wants to write a book'; and that sounds up to date enough for anybody, though it is probably twenty thousand years old.

Whatever our early forefathers did about the situation thus described, it is reasonably certain that some of them got together in the open air, marched somewhere, and ended up with a demonstration at some shrine or other appropriate and significant spot.

This kind of public witness is as old as the hills and it is still potentially the most effective means of expressing and stimulating public opinion.

It provides a real though partial answer – if only by adding legs to ideas – to those who feel the irresistible urge to do something more than register a conviction.

It breaks through the 'public meeting' barrier and communicates its message to those who seem totally impervious to the appeal to assemble together indoors. Politicians as well as parsons know the tedium of seeing nothing but the old familiar faces in their congregations.

It 'confirms the feeble knees' of those who are weak in the faith by giving to them the exhilaration of a public witness to the convictions.

The marcher is a marked man. He has nailed his colours to a mast that is plainly visible. To put it exactly in Miltonic words, the virtue of those who go in processions is no longer 'unexercised and unbreathed.'

Perhaps above all there seems to be a catholicity about the open air which defies any other environment. The banners which will be carried to Aldermaston are likely to bear many a 'strange device' and in some cases it may take some little insight to perceive the basic unity which binds together their almost infinite variety.

For those who abominate the present policies of suspicions, threats and nuclear deterrents, and have become convinced of the moral and practical rightness of unilateral repudiation of these policies – getting out like this into the open air and bearing witness to our faith and purpose is obvious common sense as well as being the least that honourably we can do.

This is the kind of justification which can be given to those who can't see what good the Aldermaston march will achieve, and who can't see the point of making an exhibition of ourselves.

There are two sorts of 'Weary Willies' who talk like this. First the clever ones who are timorous of supporting anything which smacks of a 'united front' because it will sully the 'pure radiance' of the truth as they see it.

There are the half-way houses who want to retain the American deterrent and are scared that they might find themselves walking beside a vegetarian pacifist, and the Right-wingers who are afraid that they may find a Victory For Socialism placard fluttering over their heads.

Surely the answer to these fears of compromise and blurring of the issues is that those who march to Aldermaston are not united on what positively *must* be done to secure peace on earth and they have never even suggested that they are.

They are united, however, about some things that *must not* be done, if the possibility of planning for peace is to become a reality.

They are demanding a stop to something that is evil, as a necessary step to the discovery of the right way (upon which there is the widest disagreement as yet) to start practising a policy that is good.

I'm a Christian pacifist and I'll march with any and every man and woman who sincerely opposes the H-bomb for the sake of peace and good-will, and if I can't go all the way with them it isn't because I'm afraid of compromising my own position. It's because I've got arthritis in one leg and the remains of a thrombus in the other.

The other sort are the dignified ones who hardly think it seemly to parade – especially at this season of the year and imagine that the only reaction that is certain to occur is that of ridicule.

Well, I've taken part in quite a few marches and as a matter of fact I have invariably been enheartened by the degree of respect, sometimes blossoming into a wistful admiration, that the average bystander offers to those who, even in this elementary way, seek to practise what they preach.

But what if we do make an exhibition of ourselves – a hundred thousand men and women would constitute an 'exhibit' which no Government could ignore, and the road to Aldermaston could be thronged with twice that number if every one who believes in the march takes part in it.

I would end by making a special appeal to my co-religionists of every denomination and faith to join the march; and to my fellow Christians I would add that there never was a better time at which to demonstrate for peace than at Easter which is the anniversary of the triumph of the Prince of Peace.

COME ON IN, THE FALL-OUT'S LOVELY!

Broadcaster, actor and goon Spike Milligan had his own message for the Aldermaston marchers of 1960. It was published in 'Tribune' *on April 15 1960.*

Aldermaston Marchers hear this and tremble in the foundations of your sodden Left-Wing shoes. At this very moment, if not sooner, the Milligan inter-party, espionage, phone-tapping, radio-hitting counter-espionage movement has gleaned certain information which should be imparted to you who will shortly march forth (or is is April tenth?) for the cause.

Last night I gained access to Downing Street by merely not causing a disturbance, appearing to have no desire to live, looking utterly indifferent to South Africa's death roll, and executing several Non-U turns in a U-turn street. Discreetly I crawled on to the pavement outside Number 10.

'Looking for something?' said a policeman. 'Yes,' I said, 'a new Government.'

'You won't find it here, sir, this is the old.'

I stood up.

'Who did you vote for?' I said. 'Oh, I don't vote,' he said, 'I'm one of the don't knows.'

'I thought I recognised the uniform,' I said.

'What are hinferring, madam?' (He had bad eyesight as well).

'I am suggesting that there are far too many don't knows. One day the don't knows will get in and then what will happen?'

'I don't know,' he said. 'Now move along,' and he pointed further down.

This, dear reader, was all only a cover-up while I made my way to the International Russian-controlled phone-tapping post at Number 7. I was welcomed at this door by a Russian girl athlete who put me into a cubicle.

'Just listen in on that,' she said pointing to a pair of headphones. 'It's ten roubles for three minutes. If Mac's on form you should get some pretty good copy.'

At last I'd found it, the Gossip Writer's Nirvana where Tanfield and Hickey exchange notes, here in this simple gutter in Downing Street.

THE FOLLOWING IS THE TEXT OF A TELEPHONE CONVERSATION BETWEEN THE P.M. AND HEATHCOTE AMORY:

MAC: Heathcote?

AMORY: Speaking. What are you doing up so early?

MAC: I'm worried, do you hear me? Worried!

AMORY: Is that Profit Tax hurting the book trade? Say the word and I'll take it –

MAC: No, no, no! Haven't you heard? They're marching again this Easter.

AMORY: Not the Aldermaston lot?

MAC: Yes. The first time – well, we all took it as a joke. Last year there were ten thousand of 'em and to make it even more infuriating they were all orderly. Police were powerless.

AMORY: You think that this year –

MAC: Bigger than ever.

AMORY: Say the word and I'll put a tax on marching –

MAC: No, no, no, Heathcote, no. I've already been planning an alternative march. I've been training 'em for the last three months.

AMORY: How? When? Where? Who? What? Which?

MAC: Steady, Heathcote, don't excite yourself. Remember you're a bachelor. You remember the John O' Groats to Lands End March?

AMORY: Yes, I saw it on the telly.

MAC: What may have appeared a simple publicity stunt by Bill Butlin was in fact a heavily disguised training walk by the Young Conservatives.

AMORY: Floreat Macmillan....

MAC: Ta. At this very moment ten thousand true blue Young Tories are encamped in the Vale of Healthy Hampstead disguised as out of season fair-ground attendants.

AMORY: Master!

MAC: Ta. I, Harold Macmillan, née Prime Minister, née Son of Eden, hope to turn the tide by marching in the exact opposite direction! I will march all the way by Rolls Royce.

AMORY: That should put their shares up.

MAC: Following me will be the 'Atom Bombs for Peace' group with the banner – *Strontium 90 is Good For You; Get Some Today*. Small miniature flower-clad A-bombs will be exploded en route to give festive gaiety to the occasion, and from time to time young Tory back-benchers will jump into the centre of simulated mushroom clouds with the cries of – 'Look, it doesn't hurt at all!' and/or 'Come on in, the fall-out is lovely!'

AMORY: Is that safe?

MAC: I'm not sure. Anyhow, we can afford a few Tories, the woods are full of 'em, eh? Ha ha!

AMORY: We must not take the opposition too lightly though, Mac. There's people among them who think above the waist – even higher.

MAC: Yes, blast 'em!

AMORY: Say the word, Mac, and I'll put a tax on all J. B. Priestleys.

MAC: No, no, no. You've done enough for England – to get lung cancer now costs tuppence more – well done Amory!

At this point the great British G. P. O. system working true to its ecstatic form collapsed . . . however, we had heard enough, so, friends, don't forget to march in the opposite direction to the you-know-whos!

Judith Hart

THE CHALLENGE OF POLITICS

After the initial protest came the search for a politics in which to give it continuing expression.

The three contributions that follow are indicative of the paths explored by the nuclear disarmers in their search for new politics.

Judith Hart is a journalist and Labour Member of Parliament for Lanark. In 'Tribune', *April 15 1960, she argued the case for concentrating the campaign against nuclear weapons within the Labour Party.*

Edward Thompson was editor of the 'New Reasoner', *which subsequently merged with* 'Universities and Left Review' *to become the* 'New Left Review'. *In the* 'New Reasoner', *Summer 1959, he argued for new machinery of political expression, independent of but exerting pressure on the Labour Party.*

Ralph Schoenman conceived the idea of a Committee of 100 committed to mass non-violent resistance against preparations for nuclear war. He persuaded Bertrand Russell and Michael Scott to sponsor the new organisation. In 'Peace News', *August 25 1961, he detailed his own concept of mass resistance.*

Once in every generation it comes: the catalyst of savage discontent. A single issue; but it rises to an intensity of protest which, taken at the flood, can surge into revolutionary fervour.

And the test of politicians is what they make of it. If they can successfully relate it to its wider context; if they can recognise its dynamism; if they can rise to the challenge it throws out to them – then they can capture the spirit of a whole generation and lead it forward to conquer new worlds.

Today we march from Aldermaston. And in a world which sits and watches cataclysms of mankind from comfortable chairs by the fireside, our march is some new kind of miracle. It is no weak or phoney ideal that brings men and women by coach and bus and train from towns and villages all over Britain.

This is not just London marching. It is the housewife from Glasgow. It is the doctor from Manchester, the students from Cardiff, the miner from Durham, the office worker from Edinburgh. And the force that brings them to Aldermaston is the strongest and most powerful moral purpose this generation knows.

It is a moral purpose that springs from individual conscience. I suppose that it is essentially a protest against insanity. Acceptance of Britain's nuclear weapons policy seems to us to display a pathological nostalgia for suicide: the death-wish on a mass-scale. Most of us in the Campaign came into it primarily because the H-bomb seems to us to raise new moral issues – because it threatens to destroy a whole civilisation, and to warp and cripple the human race itself. Once in it for this compelling reason, we examine its implications in more detail.

We consider the logic of the thing: partly to influence those whose conscience is imprisoned within the prison bars of prejudice and a closed mind; partly because we must reassure ourselves that we are the same ones – that our moral revulsion from the implications of nuclear weapons is soundly based in rational argument.

And so we progress from a beginning in individual morality to a conclusion which is political, in an international sense. Progress is in stages: one travels through the argument like a geometrical theorem.

It begins with the assertion of the evil of nuclear weapons. It demonstrates that Britain, by possessing them, is exposing herself to national suicide if they should ever be used, as we know they would be used if war should seem imminent – so that they offer no defence in any sense of the word. Therefore, it says, we should renounce them.

It then accepts the implications of unilateralism; which are that Britain could no longer remain a member of NATO, or of the Western defence alliance since she would have contracted out of her obligations as a member. From that position, it faces the fact that this would threaten the existence of NATO itself, and asserts that Britain would then devote her energies to the strengthening of the United Nations and to the effective creation of a UN police force to maintain world peace.

But we must recognise that in pursuing the argument this far, we have made an assumption of tremendous importance. And it is this assumption rather than the detail of the argument which is challenged by all those who oppose unilateral action by Britain.

It is the belief that co-existence, and, indeed, co-operation between the West and the Soviet Union is possible – and that if the Western defence bloc abandons its tightly knit military integration, we shall not see the Red Army walking through Europe in bloodless conquest.

A profound belief in Russia's potential aggression is the emotional basis of the nuclear deterrent theory which finds its expression in NATO. It is a belief which holds prisoner so many parlour generals. They cannot see the world of 1960 through the eyes of the young people on the Aldermaston March; their eyes are blinded by harsh memories of the past, and by their own personal experience of bitter conflict with the Communist party-line in the political and industrial battlefield in our own country.

It is easy to understand this. And, indeed, if we make a supreme effort to identify ourselves with them for a moment we can better hope to convince them that they are wrong. But it is on this rock-bottom basis of difference that we must state our case.

I believe that no sane nation – and no sane leaders of a nation – can, in today's circumstances of highly developed nuclear weapons seek to risk war by committing aggression. This seems to me to be particularly true of Russia, which is achieving such a rate of scientific and technological progress that she begins to demonstrate the superiority of a planned and Socialist economy.

For what territorial gains in Europe is she likely to risk her economic progress? And is there not more at stake for Russia than merely her prospects of improving the material standards of her people?

She must also think, in the context of what seems to be a certain degree of liberalisation and freedom of thought achieved in recent years, of justifying her Marxist philosophy in material terms. For these reasons, among others, there seems good ground for accepting the sincerity of Khrushchev's expressions of Russia's desire for peace.

But here is another deeper factor involved in this basic difference of attitude between nuclear disarmers, who accept the political and international implications of their policy, and those who distrust Russian intentions. It is the difference between a faith in the future of mankind – a profound sense of optimism springing, perhaps from some instinct for living – and what seems to be a disturbing, deeply-rooted pessimism.

It is as though those who support our present defence policy have plunged themselves into a whirlpool of despair from which there is no escape by drowning, and in which the exercise of free will and self-determination have been voluntarily surrendered.

Those of us who march are asserting our own free will and our hope for the future. And in doing so, we are demonstrating that our campaign against the bomb is not merely a negative protest; it has a profound and powerful positive content. We are committed to our positive belief in humanity. And this is perhaps the most remarkable thing of all.

For the years since the war have been years of uncommittedness.

They have been the hopeless years of intellectual withdrawal and the cult of cynicism. A mood which began with reaction against the totality of shared experience inevitable during the war, found expression in the existentialist philosophy of the Left Bank in Paris, reached its zenith – or nadir, whichever way you like to look at it – in Sam Beckett's dustbin desperation.

We saw its first breaking up in our own Angry Young Men; wild protest was a first escape-route from social detachment and self-absorption. The present protest of the beatnik is a natural follow-on to Jimmy Porter.

And now, the break-up of the cult of uncommittedness finds its expression in our Campaign. The men and women of the march care passionately about the world. They are, many of them, the same men and women who are roused to furious protest about South Africa. For it is all part of the same compassion for humanity, the same commitment to a belief in the future of man.

Because this is its true basis – extending far beyond the issue of nuclear weapons in themselves – we must see where our new readiness to commit ourselves to a cause will lead us.

Indeed, because our march from Aldermaston to Trafalgar Square represents so much more than a cry of protest about the bomb itself, it is of supreme importance – if we are to be true to ourselves and to the idealism we share – that we should begin to understand the link between morals and politics.

It needs a very real courage to accept the challenge of politics today: it needs keen perception and faith in one's own judgment to penetrate the smokescreen and apparent superficiality of party politics and come up smiling from beneath the layers of party procedure and local organisation.

The fulfilment of social morality in the modern world can be achieved only through the exercise of political power. That is the reality of morals and politics. That is, of course, why I am a member of the Labour Party: because I possess that thing so usefully summarised as a social conscience and understand that a political party, with all its irritations and frustrations, is the only means I have of giving effective expression to my ethical beliefs.

Nursing them in smug self-satisfaction at home while I watch world events shaping themselves on the television screen is uncreative. Playing my part in a political movement, seeking at the same time to persuade it that my view on some point of difference is the right view and to assist in giving it the power of government, is positive and creative.

And, of course, Socialism – the philosophy of the Labour Party – is in its broadest sense a belief of man to create for himself a society founded on exactly those moral standards which bring us all to Aldermaston.

It is probably true that politicians may be judged by their response to the challenge of politics. They have it in their power to create a new world. For so much can be done if they will recognise their own power to do it.

E. P. Thompson

THE NEW LEFT

'I am really sorry to see my countrymen trouble themselves about politics,' wrote William Blake in 1810. 'Houses of Commons and Houses of Lords appear to me to be Fools; they seem to me to be something Else besides Human Life.' And yet on the next page of his notebook he was denouncing 'the wretched State of Political Science, which is the Science of Sciences.'

We share his dilemma today. Against the vast back-cloth of nuclear promise and nuclear threat, the old political routines have lost their meaning. Mr Macmillan's business with the fur hat: Mr Gaitskell sharing the platform on NATO Day (the day after London's May Day), with M. Spaak and Mr Selwyn Lloyd: these things no longer arouse scorn, or indignation, or partisanship of any kind. They are tedious. They are 'something Else besides Human Life.' Strontium-90 is a merciless critic; it penetrates alike the specious rhetoric about a 'free community of nations,' the romantic *longeurs* of imperialism in retreat, the flatulent composure of the Fabian 'social engineer,' the bluff incompetence and moral atrophy of the 'political realists.'

And yet it is these men who hold within their control the very course of human life. And so the business of controlling *them* is indeed the 'Science of Sciences.'

It is in recognition of this fact that some members of the younger generation are beginning to take up political activity. They are doing this, not because they have clearly-formulated political objectives, but because they think it necessary to watch the politicians.

It is a difficult generation for the Old Left to understand. It is, to begin with, the first in the history of mankind to experience adolescence within a culture where the possibility of human annihilation has become an after-dinner platitude. Tommy Steele anticipated Mr Godfrey Liam by several years, in writing the appropriate hymn for NATO:

Bertrand Russell, a leading figure in the Campaign for Nuclear Disarmament, addressing a rally in Trafalgar Square

The first day there'll be lightning
The second day there'll be hail
The third daybreak there'll be a big earthquake
So brother, forward my mail.

Rock 'n roll you sinners,
Sing to save your soul –
There ain't no room for beginners
When the world is Rock 'n Roll.

It is a generation which never looked upon the Soviet Union as a weak but heroic Workers' State; but, rather, as the nation of the Great Purges and of Stalingrad, of Stalin's Byzantine Birthday and of Khrushchev's Secret Speech: as the vast military and industrial power which repressed the Hungarian rising and threw the first sputniks into space.

A generation which learned of Belsen and Hiroshima when still at elementary school; and which formed their impressions of Western Christian conduct from the examples of Kenya and Cyprus, Suez and Algeria.

A generation nourished on '1984' and 'Animal Farm,' which enters politics at the extreme point of disillusion where the middle-aged begin to get out. The young people, who marched from Aldermaston, and who are beginning, in many ways, to associate themselves with the socialist movement, are enthusiastic enough. But their enthusiasm is not for the party, or the movement, or the established political leaders. They do not mean to give their enthusiasm cheaply away to any routine machine. They expect the politicians to do their best to trick or betray them.

At meetings they listen attentively, watching for insincerities, more ready with ironic applause than with cheers of acclaim. They prefer the amateur organisation and the amateurish platforms of the Campaign for Nuclear Disarmament to the method and manner of the Left-wing professional. They are acutely sensitive to the least falsity or histrionic gesture, the 'party political' debating-point, the tortuous evasions of 'expediency.' They judge with the critical eyes of the first generation of the nuclear age.

Established sources who want to see the young people 'got hold of' and who are alarmed at the first symptoms of a self-activating socialist youth movement, have sounded the alarm. The Labour Party Executive has even appointed a committee to sit on the question of youth. But youth has been making its own inquiries; and the Labour Party Executive has not come out of them too well.

What they fail, all of them, to recognise, is that the young people who are entering political activity today are indeed ' concerned with serious politics.' Serious politics today in any worthwhile scale of human values, commences with nuclear disarmament. Those who do not understand this are either stupid (in which case they may yet be convinced); or they have become so mesmerised with political trivia, or have pushed their emotions so far down under, that they mistake the machinery of politics for the thing itself (in which case they are no longer on the Left, but are on the other side).

The young marchers of Aldermaston, despite all immaturities and individualistic attitudes, are at root more mature than their critics on the Old Left. They have understood that ' politics ' have become too serious to be left to the routines of politicians. As for ' moral and spiritual values,' what can Old Left or Old Right offer, after all?

The fourth day there'll be darkness
The last time the sun has shone,
The fifth day you'll wake up and say
The world's real gone . . . .

(Tommy Steele: ' Domesday Rock ')

In terms of traditional ' politics,' we have been living through the decade of the Great Apathy. And this has been a phenomenon common to all the highly industrialised nations, irrespective of differences in ideology and social structure. It can be traced, in part, to economic and social causes operative in East and West – the drive for ' normality ' and security in the aftermath of war, growing economic affluence (in a few favoured industrial countries), an affluence which has been co-incident with the supreme international immoralities of the Cold War and of colonial repression. Above all, it can be traced to the Cold War itself, and to its military, political, economic and ideological consequences.

But the most characteristic form of expression of this ' apathy ' has been in the sense of impotence, on the part of the individual, in face of the apparatus of the State. This has arisen, in different countries, from quite different causes; American ' Power Elite,' Russian ' Bureaucracy,' British ' Establishment,' all draw their strength from greatly different social contexts, and the attempt to press superficial resemblances too far will lead to specious conclusions. Nevertheless, if we are concerned with the formative cultural influences upon the post-war generations, then the similarities acquire significance. It is important to assess how these similarities appear to the post-war consciousness:–

1. – *The Establishment of Power.* The increasing size, complexity,

and expertise required in industrial concerns have contributed to the sense of ' anonymity ' of the large-scale enterprise, to the power of the managers, and to the sense of insignificance of the individual producer. World war, followed by cold war, and reinforced in the Soviet Union by the highly centralised economic planning of the Stalin era, further intensified these changes and helped on the process of the consolidation of immense resources at the disposal of the State.

In Britain this brought into being an unholy coming-together of the Federation of British Industries, the Trades Union Congress and Government to form a super-Establishment, which has invested its own procedures with an air of ' official ' sanctity so that the non-conformists or minority group (' unofficial ' strikers, ' proscribed ' organisations, etc.), are presented as offenders against Decency, Law and Order – a process most clearly seen at work in the treatment of the ' blue ' union in the docks, the events at Briggs Motors, and the ' official ' Court of Inquiry into the British Overseas Airways Corporation.

2. – *The Establishment of Orthodoxy*. Two factors have combined to generate a climate of intellectual conformity: first, the centralised control, either by great commercial interests or by the State itself, of the media of communication, propaganda, and entertainment, and the consequent elimination from them of minority opinions; second the ideological orthodoxies and heresy-hunting which have been a by-product of the Cold War.

In Russia this orthodoxy has been enforced by the authority of the State; but in the U.S.A. and Britain, where the forms of democracy have been preserved, the major political parties, Republican and Democrat, Conservative and Labour, endorse officially the Cold War orthodoxies of anti-Communism, NATO strategy, nuclear arms manufacture and the rest so that on the crucial issues of human survival, the electorate are presented with no effective choice.

3. – *The Establishment of Institutions*. Here the post-war generation encounter institutions which had already become ' set ' in their leadership, bureaucracy, procedures and policies, in the war or immediate post-war years. These institutions enshrine and perpetuate attitudes which have their origin in a pre-war generation, as institutions set apart from and above them.

This is notably the case with the British Labour Party, which, while it may still hold the electoral support of great numbers in the post-war generation, has failed to win the loyalty or participation of the younger electors. The younger generation have no memories of Labour as a movement of storm and protest, a movement of men struggling and sacrificing to lift themselves and their fellows out of cramping and de-humanising conditions. They were born, rather, into the world of the block vote; it is the trade union that tells them what they can do and what they can't do. They see restriction where their fathers saw mutual support. And the young socialist today is not only concerned with changing the direction of Labour Party policy; he is hostile to its integration with the rest of the Establishment, hostile to the party bureaucracy, hostile to the 'game political,' hostile to the machine itself.

These are some of the ingredients of the Great Apathy. But 'apathy' is a misleading term, confusing contradictory phenomena. On the one hand we have seen the blatant salesmanship of acquisitive materialism, and the conformists in State and Party and industry – in the U.S.A. the gaudy showcase and the great rat-race: in the U.S.S.R. the time-serving conformity of the *apparatchiks*: in Britain Mr Gaitskell's Glossy and Mr Macmillan's Opportunity State and the ethic of 'Room at the Top.' And as a concomitant of all these, a profound moral inertia, retreat from political commitment, failure to engage the idealism of youth, and a slowing down of the dynamic of social change.

On the other hand, there have been the scarcely-concealed injustices and inequalities, the increase in criminality, the social neurosis and inarticulate frustrations – dope-addicts and 'Beats,' *stilyagi*, gang conflicts and race riots.

For a multitude, East and West, 'apathy' has not been the expression of content, so much as the function of impotence. And impotence is generating its own forms of revolt, in which utter political disillusion combines with the anarchistic posturing of the isolated individual. On occasion it spills over into the frenzy of the impotent verbal assassin:

I want to run into the street,
Shouting 'Remember Vanzetti!'
I want to pour gasoline down your chimneys.
I want to blow up your galleries.
I want to burn down your editorial offices.
I want to slit the bellies of your frigid women.
I want to sink your sailboats and launches.
I want to strangle your children at their finger paintings.
I want to poison your Afghans and poodles.

(Kenneth Rexroth: 'Thou Shalt Not Kill')

The note is found among the 'beat' writers; whenever the crust breaks it can be found in Eastern Europe as well – in the cult of Hemingway, the eager acceptance of '1984,' in the stories of Hlasko; it is present in the shriller passages of John Osborne. And, in less articulate or less histrionic forms, it is found at every level of society. It is present as a mood of anti-political nausea; a nausea which extends to the very language and routines of the orthodox, whether the rituals of Marxist-Leninist ideologues or the fireside insincerities of Western tele-politicians. It is found in the obstinate resistance to the canvasser; 'there's not much to choose between 'em, they're all in it for themselves, what's the use?' It is expressed in the derisory vote of the Amalgamated Engineering Union membership, when confronted with the choice of Carron or Birch. The old routines have ceased to bring the old results. Such results as they do bring are rarely a cause for socialist congratulation.

We place the problem in this context, not because we think that such hasty impressionism is a substitute for the hard work of close political analysis; not because we incline towards the attitudes of Rexroth or of Hlasko; not because we believe that advanced industrialism itself has given rise to a 'mass society' in which the antagonism between the power elite, or state bureaucracy, and the alienated individual has superseded, in importance, class antagonisms. The water-shed of the October Revolution cannot be argued away; and we believe that, in an atmosphere of relaxed international tension, the Soviet Union and Eastern Europe will prove to be the area of expanding liberty and human fulfilment, whereas the West, unless transformed by a strong democratic and revolutionary socialist movement, will prove to be the area of encroaching authoritarianism.

Moreover – and the reservation is of great importance – whereas in the capitalist powers, and especially U.S.A., great private interests find the maintenance of tension and arms production profitable, in the East no comparable vested interests in the cold war are to be found. While at the rubbing edges of the 'Two Camps' – Jordan or Tibet, Albania or Turkey – the actions of military strategists and politicians, East and West, can be equally fraught with danger, nevertheless it remains true that the 'natural' economic and social pressures in the East lead towards a détente, whereas in the West we are faced with the inertia of the 'permanent war economy.'

But the assertion of democracy in the Communist area cannot take place without a hundred contests with the entrenched bureaucracy, its institutions and ideology. And, equally, the regeneration of the Western socialist movement cannot take place without a fundamental break with the policies and orthodoxies of the past decade. And this two-pronged offensive is (it becomes increasingly clear) carrying the left Socialist in the West, and the dissident Communists to liberal social-democracy. It represents, rather, a rediscovery of common aims and principles, obscured during the violent era of the Third International.

This does not constitute a conversion of sections of the Western labour movement to Communist orthodoxy, nor of disillusioned Communists to liberal social-democracy .It represents, rather, a rejection of both orthodoxies; and the emergence of a New Left which, while it draws much from both traditions, stands apart from the sterile antagonisms of the past, and speaks for what is immanent within both societies. It champions a new internationalism, which is not that of the triumph of one camp over the other, but the dissolution of the camps and the triumph of the common people.

It is the bankruptcy of the orthodoxies of the Old Left, and particularly their imprisonment within the framework of cold war ideology and strategy, which has contributed to the characteristic political consciousness of the post-war generation – the sense of impotence in the face of the Establishment. Because there has been during the past decade no determined and effective grouping, with a clear internationalist perspective, challenging these orthodoxies, has given way to disillusion, and disillusion to apathy. Now that such groupings are appearing, in different forms, in a dozen different countries, East and West, the Establishment immediately appears less firmly based; apathy appears as a less formidable phenomenon; and a certain identity of aim is discovered.

First, these groupings find a common enemy not only in the tensions of the cold war, but also in the strategic postulates and partisan ideology of the war. The neutralist position is expressed in the diplomacy of the uncommitted Afro-Asian nations, Yugoslavia, etc., it is also a spreading heresy in the Communist and Western world. It is the first sin of ' revisionism ' to come under attack; it was the supreme crime of Nagy and of Harich. It is the neutralist implication of the Campaign for Nuclear Disarmament which provokes the hostility of the Establishment (Mr Gaitskell, Mr Bevan, and all) in Britain. As the pressure grows greater in one ' camp,' so the response will grow greater in the other.

It must be the first task for any New Left in Britain to propagate and to deepen, in the labour movement and in the nuclear disarmament campaign, not the mere sentiment of neutralism, but the internationalist outlook of active neutrality. We must seek to bring our people to an awareness of their key position in world affairs, by fostering a far wider understanding, not only of the outlook of the colonial and Asian peoples, but also of the potential strength of ' revisionist ' and democratic forces within the Communist world.

Second, these groupings find a common problem in gaining access to channels of communication to people, despite control over the cultural apparatus by the State, the party, or commercial interests; and over the organisations of the labour movement by the party bureaucracies. This tends to keep the new groupings isolated and to emphasise their ' intellectual ' character. But their importance as growing-points should not be underestimated.

The problem differs greatly from one country to another. In France our comrades contest with an erratic and vicious censorship. There they present themselves as a distinct party (the Left Socialist Union) with little electoral influence but with widely influential journals (notably ' France-Observateur '). In Italy, the ' New Left ' tendency is to be found among elements within both the Socialist and Communist Parties, and is expressed in more than one serious theoretical journal. In Russia and in much of Eastern Europe our comrades press against the barriers of editorial inertia, and contest with State orthodoxy in a hundred tortuous ways; in China and in Viet-Nam they are being ' re-educated ' in the communes and on the dams – a process which may not prove as one-sided as their educators hope.

In Britain, the democratic forms are unimpaired, but access to the means of communication becomes increasingly difficult – when the media of television and press are largely tuned by the Establishment and are closed to the sustained propagation of minority opinions. Channels of communication within the traditional labour movement are sluggish and obstructed by the bureaucracy. The problem presents itself as one of constructing (however painfully slow the process may seem – though steady progress *is* being made) an *alternative* ' cultural apparatus,' which by-passes the mass media and the party machinery, and which opens up direct channels between significant socialist groupings inside and outside the labour movement.

Third, there is taking place within these groupings a renaissance of socialist theory. It would be premature to attempt to define a unified and consistent body of ideas by which the New Left can be identified in any country. The laboratory work is still continuing, in journals, clubs and splinter parties, in sociological theses and in novels, in discussions in cafés, communes, workshops, trade union meetings.

It would be possible to trace a recurring pattern in Communist post-1956 ' revisionism ' – the humanist revolt, the rejection of dogmatic in favour of empirical methods of analysis, opposition to authoritarian and paternalist forms of organisation, the critique of determinism, etc. But this would tell us more about the shedding of old illusions and the re-valuation of old traditions, than about the affirmation of the enduring and the discovery of the new. It would tell us nothing about the crucial question: the confluence of the dissident Communist impulse with the left socialist tradition of the West and with the post-war generation. It is at this point of confluence that the New Left can be formed.

Nineteen-fifty-six marks the watershed. In the first place, since 1956, there has been a world-wide and continuing movement of Communist dissidence which has not entered into the worn paths of traumatic anti-Communism, God-That-Failedism, Encounterism, and the rest; but which has, on the contrary, sought to affirm and develop the humane and libertarian features of the Communist tradition.

The resilience and maturity of this heresy, which – excluded from the Communist Parties – has refused to lie down and die, or to cross to the 'other camp,' but which has instead struck independent roots in the labour movement, interposing itself between the orthodox Communist apparatus and the non-Communist Left – this has aroused the particular fury of ideologues of 'World Marxist Review,' Indeed, in certain countries it would be possible to identify the New Left by saying that it stands aside from the traditional contest between Social-Democratic and Communist orthodoxy; and looks forward to socialist re-unification, not through some formal alliance of incompatibles, but as a result of the displacement of the ruling bureaucracies in both.

But we should go further. If there is, as yet, no unified theory of the New Left, there are many common pre-occupations. There is no prescribed 'road to Socialism'; but Socialism remains an international theory, with an international language. Confronted by the authoritarianism and anti-intellectualism of the Stalinist deviant of Marxism, Communist dissidence has broken with its scholastic framework and is subjecting the entire catechism to an empirical critique. But at the same time, confronted by the idiocies of the Cold War and the facts of power within Western 'over-developed societies,' a taut radical temper is arising among the post-war generation of socialists and intellectuals in the West.

In the exchange between the two a common language is being discovered, and the same problems are being thrust forward for examination: the problem of political power and of bureaucratic degeneration; the problem of economic power and of workers' control; the problems of decentralisation and of popular participation in social control. There is the same re-discovery of the notion of a socialist community; in Britain the Fabian prescription of a competitive Equality of Opportunity is giving way, among socialists, before the re-discovery of William Morris's vision of a Society of Equals; in the Communist world the false community of the authoritative collective is under pressure from the voluntary, organic community of individuals, which, despite all the inhumanities of the past two decades, has grown up within it. There is, East and West, the same renewal of interest in the 'young Marx'; the same concern with humanist propositions; the same reassertions of moral agency, and of individual responsibility within the flow of historical events.

The New Left has little confidence in the infallibility, either of institutions or of historical processes. A true socialist community will not be brought into being by legislative manipulation and top-level economic planning alone. Socialism must commence with existing people; it must be built by men and women in voluntary association. The work of changing peoples' values and attitudes and the summoning up of aspirations to further change by means of utopian critiques of existing society, remains as much a duty of socialists as the conquest and maintenance of working-class power.

At every stage, before, during and after the conquest of power, the voluntary participation of the people must be enlisted, and the centres of power must themselves, wherever possible, be broken up. The New Left is made up of revolutionary socialists; but the revolution to which they look forward must entail not only the conquest but also the dismantling of State power. They are socialist theorists who distrust the seductive symmetry of socialist theory, and revolutionaries who are on their guard against the dogmatic excesses and the power-drives of the professional revolutionary.

Ralph Schoenman

MASS RESISTANCE IN MASS SOCIETY

In 1954 Professor H. H. Wilson wrote an essay called *The Dilemma of the Obsolete Man.* In this essay Wilson argued that the values derived from liberal, democratic and socialist traditions were no longer operative and that those who laid claim to them were obsolete men. I believe this essay and the writings which preceded it to be of critical importance. Any serious examination of the institutions which characterise our societies demonstrates the extent to which the assumptions we make about them are out of keeping with their actual operation. Power is concentrated and in Western societies it is private.

The large oil corporations have leased to them over a quarter of the total land area of the continental United States and this model is evidenced in the way decisions are made. Vast interlocking directorates control production and absorb the formal institutions through which conventional theory assumes decisions to be arrived at. Intimately related to this network of private and concentrated power is control over the means of communication and the effective educators of our societies: television, newspapers, and cinema.

The active organisation of power is not confined to national boundaries. Control of capital by American cartels is such that a determining degree of ownership is maintained involving the economic life of countries around the world. Britain, for example, could never survive a simple American decision to shift its sterling holdings to another currency such as Marks or Francs. I believe that in fundamental ways the Cold War has served as a Metternich programme on the part of the West, designed to create the climate and the ideological myths necessary to prevent serious challenge to the power of the vast corporations whose control over planetary resources is maintained at the expense of the agony and starvation of its population in large.

It cannot be emphasised strongly enough that the American economy has a margin of forty per cent waste, that it fails to expand at all if the economic plant is placed against the wholesale destruction of energy resources. We have spent two out of three dollars on war and its material for a quarter of a century in the United States. Should peace break out, the effect on our institutional life would be such that the country would experience an upheaval dwarfing the depression of the 1930s. It is obviously possible, in principle, to plan the resources of the United States for production and for non-wasteful ends. But not without profound and radical alteration of the institutional life in a society so conditioned, so obdurate in its hysterical insistence that its violent world is sane, and so possessed by the controllers of this planet's wealth, that they consider their own slum-ridden society benefited by the preservation of these economic and power arrangements.

It should be patently clear that the nature of the conflict with the Soviet Union has nothing to do with an ideological preference for liberal values or civil liberties. The United States is as monolithic and autocratic a society as is likely to be produced. We must not be misled by the ability on the part of the controllers to substitute total ostracism for internment camps. This has been made possible solely by the glut of resources which enables people to be bought as opposed to their being crudely eliminated. Overt coercion, however, is now built into American institutional life and it ramifies throughout the society. It affects work, travel, study and creative activity. It conditions a fear of ideas and an intolerance that has eliminated serious communication. The dissident is rather like a Salvation Army man in a large city, walking with a signboard, and as relevant as the vegetarian party of California. We have created a concentration camp for the mind.

I believe that we must come to understand how ruthless a society the United States has become and, in particular, the manner in which the controllers require the military crisis they perpetuate in order to retain their hold. I lay stress on the United States because it is clear that those of us who are concerned to develop a movement of resistance to nuclear war must have an effective understanding of the actual basis of the power struggle being conducted by the two monolithic Powers.

There is also a more fundamental reason which bears on the arguments advanced by Professor Wilson. Our dilemma follows not only because democratic institutions have been emptied of content; or because power has become concentrated to the point of their total absorbtion. It follows from the fact that the mass society is now a totalitarian society. This latter fact represents, to my mind, far more the nature of vast industrial technology than it does ideology. It is as true of Britain as it is of the United States or the Soviet Union. In these countries individuals find vast impersonal institutions in which they are absorbed like ciphers. More depressingly, these institutions feed and breed men for quiescence. The efficient operation of a highly ordered institution, whether private or public, rests on a man who does not question ends, make demands, or display the characteristics of one not disposed to guide his manner to the dictates of the organisation he inhabits or of its bureaucracy.

It becomes clear that even were private power rendered public, the central difficulties will not be resolved with respect to individual values or the content of civil liberties. Power will remain remote, decisions impersonal, and the nature of individual participation in their being reached, minimal. The tremendous network of institutions, pressures, and the ordered and impersonal characteristics of the societies we have, substitute masses for publics. Apart from the fact that Parliament does not have power, it is so removed from the active life of people that it has decorative meaning at best and increasingly falls into open contempt.

I believe that Orwell understood these societies in an important way when he pointed to their apolitical character. A vital politics involves a clear ability to effect events and requires serious institutional expression for a common programme. We are inhabiting societies where decisions are administrative and are not seriously political because the areas of choice are peripheral.

If we are ever to understand the possibilities for large-scale civil disobedience, it will follow from a careful evaluation of what has happened to our public world and what has shaped the people in it. The overwhelming helplessness people experience, their isolation and their option for private solutions reflects the way we are crippling people in mass society. We are taking from them the ability to act independently or to relate the world around them to their own experience. Regimentation always entails degradation because the adulthood of people is compromised. Their confidence in themselves as individuals is removed when they afastened in a mesh of circumstances which fails to define them as autonomous creatures.

I believe that what we have created in Britain in the Committee of 100 is the first serious effort in Western society to enable people to reclaim their public right. I should have thought it quite impossible to challenge the super-state, the organised society and its inhumanity, had that inhumanity not exposed itself in so stark a manner as to threaten an imminent and total annihilation. During the Second World War an Italian pilot parachuted into a German concentration camp. He got into a queue of people herded towards the gas chambers. He told them that it was not within his power to prevent their dying, but he felt it important that they did not die without hope. We discuss our children and friends in terms of stripping off their skin, burning them and covering them with festering sores. That is what kill-ratios and megatonnage mean. We must seek to enable people to retain their humanity, their responsibility to Enrico Seleni for carrying the human conscience.

One of the most difficult things to make people see is the manner in which the most extraordinarily horrible things are masked in form. Societies cloak the naked violence involved in our production. We will be exposing it when we show that authority must set up vast camps to cope with our number because we address ourselves to the unlimited horror of our equivalents of Buchenwald and Auschwitz: Aldermaston, Polaris, NATO.

The critical point that I wish to make is that the covering of the planet with a fantastic network of rocket bases, the full direction of the technology of industrial societies for murderous production, make explicit the active values – the unvarnished character of our present social arrangement.

I advise this movement never to forget this when considering how to conduct the struggle. Never forget that we must expose the fraud of these institutions; never forget that we cannot rely on them for communication with masses of men. That which they convey involves a reflection of their function and will distort. Often when reading the homilies of professional liberals, whether inside or outside the movement, I feel like addressing a Message to the Meek. Consider. Were these the 1930s, and were the concentration camps going up with people being herded into them, would we gather around and say, 'What pavement shall we sit on? What building shall we surround?'

Our situation is even more desperate. That is why we cannot afford the luxury of caution or respectability. The responsible people have their fingers on the buttons.

The following task is before the Committee of 100: It must document and disseminate the data establishing the moment-to-moment urgency, the accidents. This communication of the case must be systematic and on large scale. The Committee must prepare, while it does this, a national movement which can launch frequent actions and which can sustain those undertaken. We must have local demonstrations all over the country. We must learn to use our vast numbers in waves so that a base like Polaris will suffer one thousand demonstrators every fortnight. Above all, we must be clear that we are arguing by example, that we are displaying a method which enables people to affect and to effect events. If this is to be done we must realise that we are conducting a resistance movement. We are seeking to obstruct systematically to the point where the authorities have to give way.

It is not good enough to have a series of dramatic but isolated incidents. It is not good enough for us even to achieve ten thousand sitting down if we then go off for three months to puzzle out another objective. I have tried to argue that these mass societies have stripped us of democratic responses or rights. I wish to see understood that the mass media, statements in courts, the entire reliance on the institutions of the closed society, will never serve as the basis for reaching people; for these institutions legitimise and we must expose the fraud. Our confrontation effects the tearing of the veil.

Demonstrations must not end with the sit-down. Otherwise after two days of headlines and a certain amount of inconvenience for the courts the authorities are in the clear. We must begin to pledge people in their thousands to carry the challenge further. If ten thousand have to be carried into court where they refuse to say a mumbling word; if ten thousand have to be jailed – then we shall realise the meaning of civil disobedience and I dare say so will the makers of Bombs.

Our political theorists are strutting in vain over cadavers for our political institutions are empty. The model of our objective should be the General Strike. We are not a political party. We have no intention of providing a civil service or an alternative body of administrators. We have precise demands which must be pressed on authority. They will acquiesce or face national disruption. There shall undoubtedly be a host of political consequences of our resistance. We must not be deluded by them. If we hand over our consciences to any political party we will be betrayed. There is no party, no bureaucracy, and no authority which may not outrage our most fundamental values.

We must never act without clear comprehension of the context of our struggle. In mass society human beings are chained by institutions. It is not out of any formal anarchism but out of a radical consciousness that civil disobedience must return to individuals the prospect of a vital participation in the public world. Our responsibility is to develop a movement which does not so much aspire to power as it does to present *any* authority with a populace conscious of its ability to act on its most precious values.

Even if individuals are associated with political parties when the movement is stronger, the heart of our movement is resistance. If our values are outraged by any government, that government will find tens of thousands prepared to go to prison on behalf of those values. We must give no hostages through dependence on a particular régime. We must constitute the articulate expresssion of an active populace, alive to human right and to human responsibility.

Short of this Eichmann stands for Everyman.

Sir Herbert Read

DISOBEDIENCE

Sir Herbert Read, the elder statesman of anarchism, wrote this defence of civil disobedience on the eve of a Committee of 100 demonstration against Polaris. It was published in ' Peace News ' *on January 20 1961.*

The case for civil disobedience is the case of the individual conscience against the authority of government. So long as government is absolute and tyrannical there are few reasonable people who would not admit the right of the individual to revolt when his conscience is outraged by a power that has no respect for humanity.

The problem becomes more difficult when the government is a democratic one, and claims to represent the will of the people. But even democratic governments represent only a majority of the people, and sometimes (as in our own country) by a very small margin.

The case for civil disobedience in a democratic state is not so obvious as it is in a tyrannical state, but modern democracy is a very impure institution. Its authority rests on an election in which many diverse and inconsistent policies are presented to the public, and any one vote may be determined by one of a hundred issues. There has never been a vote on the unequivocal issue of peace or war, and certainly never a vote on whether our country should commit itself to the manufacture and use of atomic weapons.

But even if there had been such a vote and a majority was in favour of such a policy, I should still be prepared to disobey the authority of a government that proposed to use such weapons against our fellow-men.

I believe there are convincing strategical and political arguments for nuclear disarmament, but I will not use them on this occasion. They are known to most of you and have been expounded with more political acumen than I can claim to possess. My intention to commit an act of civil disobedience in opposition to an official policy that contemplates atomic warfare is neither strategical nor political: it is instinctive.

War itself is instinctive. Its immediate causes are economic, but governments would not be able to delude their people into aggressive and murderous acts but for certain frustrations common to us all – emotional tensions caused in us by social conventions that are basically an aspect of the struggle for survival. Frustration automatically arouses aggressive impulses – this is one of the most established of all psychological laws.

To survive without war the society of nations must so arrange its economy and morals that frustration is not entailed with mutual danger to its constituent members, but that is a long-term policy for statesmen, and meanwhile the stockpile of atomic weapons increases. Stupid and bewildered men rise to power and the whole fate of humanity is attached to a very delicate trigger.

To have reached this state of imminent peril is in itself an unparalleled disaster for which the statesmen and scientists of the world have forfeited all moral authority. Not one of us has any longer any faith in political action. The more conferences and committees we arrange and attend, the farther away we seem to get from any immediate and practical intention to disarm.

This stalemate must be broken, but it will never be broken by rational argument. There are too many right reasons for wrong actions on both sides. It can be broken only by instinctive action. An act of disobedience is instinctive: civil disobedience is or should be collectively instinctive – a revolt of the instincts of man against the threat of mass destruction.

Instincts are dangerous things to play with, but that is why, in the present desperate situation, we must play with instincts. The apathetic indifference of the majority of people to the very real threat of universal destruction is partly due to a lack of imagination, but the imagination does not function in the present situation because it is paralysed by fear in its sub-conscious sources.

We must release the imagination of the people so that they become fully conscious of the fate that is threatening them, and we can best reach their imagination by our actions, by our fearlessness, by our willingness to sacrifice our comfort, our liberty, and even our lives to the end that mankind shall be delivered from pain and suffering and universal death.

Alan Sillitoe

SUNDAY NIGHT AND MONDAY MORNING

The author of Saturday Night and Sunday Morning *contributed this account of his participation in a Committee of 100 sit-down to* 'Sanity', *October 1961.* 'Sanity', *explained that he sat down on Sunday night and was fined on Monday morning.*

I do not find it easy to say why I went to the Committee of 100 demonstration in Trafalgar Square on September 17, especially in a short article. Too many fragmented reasons come to me at the same time.

It is no use me saying that I *obstructed the police* because I didn't want to die for Berlin and the West Germans, or that I sat down because I don't believe any nation should possess that symbol of supreme power and destruction, the hydrogen bomb. These reasons are so obvious that I regard them as emotional, and therefore not reasons at all.

The anti-bomb campaign is, obviously, a political movement. It is also disenfranchised and, as such, is revolutionary, more dangerous than if it had a couple of hundred MPs in Parliament – which would make it useless. The longer it remains unrepresented the more certain will be its complete victory.

I imagine Mr Gaitskell regrets now that he did not abide by the Scarborough decision so that he could perhaps have tried to kill unilateralism in a more effective (though in the end less dramatic) way. He missed his chance of being known as the saviour of the old order. If no major political party accepts the CND voice overwhelmingly and unconditionally we may be on hand for another 'ten days that shook the world,' in which even the all-seeing eye of a helicopter will be blinded at the crowds in the streets.

Being without Parliamentary representation the only way to air our democratic rights is by demonstration. Apart from the fact that I abhor symbols of extreme power such as the bomb, I went to the sit-down to get arrested because even this outlet was being denied to me. As it turned out, the price of democracy (which should be free) was comparatively cheap at two pounds and a night in the police station.

This society will sell anything, even democracy. It will, however, become a seller's market, and the price will increase a great deal, as some of our political prisoners of the Committee of 100 already know.

Many people believe that war is a force of nature, and the father of progress (and all that), but this is the philosophy of animals, of those who lack intelligence and faith, and man's beginning can only date from the time when the illnesses of war are brought under control. Since 1945 nature has delivered an ultimatum: abolish war, or get blown to pieces.

Supporters of the CND and the Committee of 100 listen to this voice, and relay it to the people of this country. None of the present political leaders dare tune in to it. They have neither the courage, nor the vision, to accept the credo of unilateral nuclear disarmament, because acceptance would mean that they, with their old values, would be out of office and power.

Someone writing to the 'Daily Telegraph' said he thought Britain was going soft with pacifism, and that pacifism had been the cause of the last war in that the Nazi Germans had thought their chances were good because the Oxford students had forsaken king and country. Simple people have only history to guide them, while those with more complex minds can also draw on vision and intelligence.

Everyone who sat down in Trafalgar Square did so for political reasons, and in so doing they threaten (or would if there were enough of them) the basis on which the present political life of this country stands. Without armaments and nuclear weapons we could only survive as a Socialist country. With them, we shall not. These are the cold emotionless issues that got me into Trafalgar Square.

OFFICIAL ENGLAND VERSUS RADICAL ENGLAND

By the nature of the courses of action they advocate, which run quite contrary to the courses chosen by the Government, nuclear disarmament campaigners – and particularly those avowedly engaged in civil disobedience campaigns – have frequently brushed with the law.

The Old Bailey Secrets Trial of February 1962 was the most spectacular of a series of legal dramas. Six members of the Committee of 100 were charged with violating the Official Secrets Act by conspiring together to enter Wethersfield air base for a purpose prejudicial to the safety and interests of the state. Official and Radical England were in direct confrontation.

The following account of the trial is pieced together from ' Peace News ' *reports and editorial comment.*

' All persons having any business to do with my Lords the Queen's Justices let them draw nigh and give their attendance. God Save the Queen!'

The Judge, Mr Havers, in red and white ermine and a wig walks in unassumingly. The other learned members of the bar bewigged and gowned bow low in deference.

The spectators in the steeply sloped gallery look down into the court. Best wood panelling everywhere. The prisoners sit in the wooden dock – five young men and a young woman. Prison warders sit immediately behind them.

On the ground level of the Court, immediately below the dock, is a long table. The instructing solicitor for the defence and his assistants sit on one side, the police (in plain clothes) on the other. Behind them, the courtroom slopes upwards. To the right with their backs towards the spectators, the Attorney-General, the barristers, law students and other privileged persons. To the left, the jury: ten men and two women.

Facing the defendants and dominating the Court sits the Judge, Mr. Justice Havers. His glasses are ' squared off ' on top and he looks constantly over the top of them. He sits slightly aslant his enormous high-back wooden chair. His face shows traces of humour.

The first session of Regina versus Committee of 100 opened late at about 11.30 on Monday, February 12. (The murder case that preceded it had gone on longer than was expected.) Before the jury were sworn in the Attorney-General rose, and held up a leaflet which he said was being distributed in the vicinity of the court. It was entitled ' Regina versus the Committee of 100 ', and was in his submission prima facie evidence of criminal contempt of court. (The leaflet had a reproduction of the sketch of Wethersfield base. It accused the Government of not applying the law impartially to all the members of the Committee and preferring to prosecute six individuals. The Committee, it stated, was proud of the Wethersfield demonstration and determined that this kind of resistance would continue on a still larger scale).

The Judge agreed that this was prima facie evidence of very serious criminal contempt. The jury would be asked if they had seen or read the leaflet before being empanelled. But none of the jury had seen or read the leaflet. They were sworn-in, after several objections, and the trial commenced. Once again the Attorney-General rose.

He is a big man. His face is very full and red and his mouth turns down at the corners. He obviously attended ' a really *good* school.'

' This is not,' said the Attorney-General, ' a political prosecution. The accused are not being prosecuted for an offence of a political character or on account of any views they may hold. They are being prosecuted for an offence on account of their conduct which, the prosecution submits, amounted to the commission of a criminal offence.'

The Attorney-General explained carefully the offences with which the accused were charged. It was alleged that they had conspired together to enter a prohibited place, Wethersfield air base, on December 9, 1961, for a purpose prejudicial to the safety and interest of the state. They had also conspired, together with persons unknown, to incite others to enter the base for such a purpose. They were therefore charged with two offences against section one of the Official Secrets Act of 1911.

On December 6, 1961, the Committee's premises in Goodwin Street and the homes of five of the accused had been searched by the police. A large number of documents had been found. Some were being used as exhibits by the prosecution. The bundle of 80 exhibits in photostat form were then handed to members of the jury. Some of the exhibits were several pages long. They included Committee minutes, leaflets, extracts from the diary of one of the accused, notes and jottings, and a list of people who had attended Michael Randle's sister's 21st birthday party.

Minutes of the first meeting of the Committee in October, 1960, showed that its purpose from the start had been to organise civil disobedience – 'which is another way of saying, breaking the law.' A Working Group was set up at this first meeting to consider various projects for civil disobedience and the legal penalties involved. Randle, Dixon and Hatton had all been founder members of the Committee and present at its first meeting. The others had joined later. All of them were also members of the Working Group.

The Attorney-General then read passages from a policy memorandum, Exhibit 24:

> 'Civil disobedience is an unusual and extreme measure to take especially in a more or less democratic society. It is made necessary because the situation we face is perilous in the extreme. Even under democracy civil disobedience may be called for in a situation of great urgency or where human rights are being violated.'

Another memorandum showed that the Committee had from the start contemplated obstructing nuclear weapons establishments. The Attorney also read extracts from the Committee leaflet *Act or Perish* which called for a movement of non-violent resistance to nuclear weapons and all weapons of mass destruction and accused the Governments of East and West of exposing the peoples of the world to appalling peril.

'Respect for the law,' the Attorney-General read on, 'is important and only a very profound conviction can justify actions which flout the law. It is generally admitted that, in the past, many such actions have been justified. Christian martyrs broke the law, and there can be no doubt that majority opinion at that time condemned them for doing so.'

The Attorney-General looked up from the exhibits: 'There you have it in their own words, that their intention was to "flout the law".'

He now turned his attention to the events directly leading up to the Wethersfield demonstration. Minutes were produced to show that all the accused had been party to the plans and had indeed played a major part in organising it. The Court would hear later that no less than 20,000 of the leaflet entitled 'Mass Resistance' had been distributed and 40,000 of the 'General Briefing for Wethersfield' which contained a map of the base and stated specifically that the intention was to ground all aircraft and demand the reclaiming of the base for civilian purposes.

The accused might well agree that they had done all this but argue that their actions were not prejudicial to the safety of the state. He would call Air Commodore Magill, the Director of Operations at the Air Ministry, to prove that Wethersfield was occupied by United

States Air Force squadrons assigned to the Supreme Allied Command, Europe, and had a vital part to play in the defence of Britain and other NATO countries.

The natural consequence of putting this airfield out of action, said Sir Reginald, would be to impair the defence of Britain.

He quoted from the judgment in a case during the first world war in which the Judge had ruled that 'Those who are responsible for national security must be the sole judges of what the national security requires.' That judgment was in no way binding but he hoped that the jury would give it due consideration.

Mrs. Allegranza had said when arrested: 'I do not agree my actions are prejudicial to the security of the state. On the contrary I think that the state's action is contrary to the interests of the people who live in it.'

'The accused,' said Sir Reginald, 'may be completely and utterly sincere in their beliefs but we are not concerned with that but with the facts.'

Deliberately to do something to immobilise any part of our defence, a ship or an aircraft, was in his submission, seeking to do something prejudicial to the safety and interests of the state.

This was the end of day one. At the committal stage of the trial the defendants had said that their defence would be that their actions were not prejudicial to the safety and interest of the state. The prosecution were now attempting to have this ruled out of order.

Bail was granted to all the defendants after they had given an assurance that they would not take part in or encourage any demonstration or distribution of literature in the precincts of the Old Bailey.

When the trial recommenced Pat Pottle announced that he would defend himself.

The Attorney-General concluded his case. There were three things for the jury to decide.

1. Had the accused agreed to try to enter and get others to enter Wethersfield air base?

2. What did they intend to do having entered the base? In his submission this was clearly to block and immobilise it.

3. Was this purpose prejudicial to the safety and interest of the state? Again in his submission any interference with the defence system of the country must obviously be so.

'You may perhaps wonder,' the Attorney-General concluded, 'why it is that only these six are in the dock and why it is others have not also been charged. In the submission of the prosecution these are the organisers and they bear a heavy responsibility.'

Chief Inspector Stratton of the Special Branch was the first prosecution witness. He looked neat and confident as he stepped into the witness box and took the oath. On November 27, 1961, he said, he had gone to the Committee Office at Goodwin Street. Randle had been at lunch but Dixon, who was there, said he was in charge during Randle's absence. While he was there he heard Chandler answering the telephone and giving details of the Wethersfield demonstration.

Allegranza was also in the office and had answered queries about the demonstration from people who came into the office and given them copies of the leaflet. Next day he and others had kept watch on the office and had seen Pottle and Allegranza putting leaflets into envelopes.

Inspector Stratton also told of the raid on the Committee office on December 6 and the subsequent arrest on December 8 of Hatton, Chandler, Dixon, Allegranza and Randle.

Pottle had evaded arrest and had not been arrested until February 6.

Jeremy Hutchinson, QC, for the defence, asked if Mr Stratton had been informed of the Committee's activities.

The Inspector paused. At first, he said, he had been kept fully informed. Lately the Committee had not been so forthcoming.

Did the Inspector realise that he was on the Committee press list? – He did not.

Did he realise that the Essex police had been informed of the Wethersfield demonstration? The Judge interrupted. A witness, he said, must only give first-hand information. Mr Stratton looked distinctly less composed now.

He agreed that one of the purposes of the Committee's demonstrations was to put forward the facts for the public.

'Did you agree with those facts?' – No.

'Have you made any kind of study about nuclear weapons or their results?'

The Attorney-General interrupted. 'This cannot be relevant... any more than it can be relevant for accused to give their views on the matter.'

The Court was silent. The crucial issue had come up. Would the Judge rule out any evidence which challenged the Government's defence policy?

Mr Hutchinson: In my submission these persons are charged under the section which uses the words 'in a manner prejudicial to the state.' Therefore the jury must find out what their purpose was.

The Judge said the witness was not an expert on nuclear matters and that his opinion was therefore irrelevant. Mr Hutchinson then agreed to keep these questions for the expert witnesses he would be calling later. The Judge nodded.

Neither he nor the Attorney-General objected that these experts and their evidence would be irrelevant.

Had the key issue then been slipped in and decided upon so unobtrusively?

Mr Hutchinson continued questioning Inspector Stratton: 'From all the documents in the case before the jury, there is absolutely nothing to show that any of these accused ever set out to obtain secret information in order to pass it on to the enemy or anything like that?' – No.

'Or obtain secret information of any kind?' – That is right.

'They did not set out to injure this country or assist any hostile power....'

ATTORNEY-GENERAL: 'Isn't that a matter of opinion?'

THE JUDGE: 'Yes. You will have to consider whether to immobilise a base would be injurious to this country.'

It was now Pat Pottle's turn to cross-examine.

He stood up, impressively solid; a thick wadge of hair jutting out like a sunshade over his forehead.

'Mr. Stratton, you say that you went to the Committee Office in Goodwin Street on November 26?' – Yes.

'You were invited to stay there to wait for Mr Randle?' Inspector Stratton agreed, after some discussion that he had remained by courtesy of the Committee.

Pat's voice rose:

'You could have been told to go outside and wait in the street in the rain. But people were good enough to allow you to stay and you made use of this opportunity to get information?'

Pat then questioned him about how much he could see from the road looking into an office on the second floor through windows with wire netting on the outside. He then went on to deal with his own arrest on February 6.

'You told the Court, Mr Stratton, that you arrested me in Kingsway as I got out of a taxi. How did you know I would be there?'

Justice Havers intervened with words that were to become very familiar in the next few days: 'You can't ask that.'

But Pat did manage to elicit from Mr. Stratton the fact that he had publicly announced that he would give a press conference on February 6 at Kingsway Hall.

'No further questions, my Lord.' Pat sat down.

Inspector Stratton was followed by another policeman. Detective-Constable Peter Toye said that on December 8 he had attended a Press Conference in a pub in Tudor Street. Randle in answer to questions had said that the Official Secrets Act was a bluff and use of it would be against civil liberties.

'Did he say anything about climbing over fences?' – It was one of the Attorney-General's understudies who was examining.

The constable thumbed slowly through his notebook.

'Yes. He said something about getting over a fence in Suffolk.' Randle began to sound like a steeplechaser (Wethersfield is in Essex). The prosecuting Counsel laughed uneasily. No doubt the constable had very full notes, he said, some of them not relevant to the present case.

The three other policemen who were called were Sgt. Reginald Oakes of the Special Branch, P.C. Alex Saward and the Assistant Chief Constable of Essex, Mr John Nightingale. All gave evidence of the events at Wethersfield. In reply to questions Mr Nightingale agreed that the Committee had written to the Chief Constable of Essex some days before the demonstration informing him of what was planned. But they had known details before the letter was received.

Then came the star witness. Air Commodore Magill, Director of Operations at the Air Ministry – called to give evidence to convince the jury that the demonstration if it had been carried out as planned, would have been prejudicial to the safety and interest of the state.

The Air Commodore was in uniform. He held himself very erect.

On December 9, he said, answering the Attorney-General, Wethersfield was occupied by squadrons of the United States Air Force, assigned to the Supreme Allied Commander Europe. The planes were vital to the defence of Britain and other countries in NATO.

THE ATTORNEY-GENERAL: 'What is the position with regard to their readiness?' – They are combat ready and at constant alert.

'Ready to take off at any time?' – Yes.

'In the event of an emergency how would their effectiveness be affected if they were prevented from taking off?' – Any interference with the ability of those aircraft to take off would gravely prejudice their operational effectiveness.

Answering Mr Hutchinson, Air Commodore Magill said the squadrons there were not part of the Strategic Air Command. From time to time the aerodrome had an open day when the public were allowed to visit it.

MR HUTCHINSON: 'What happens to the aircraft on open day. Would there be interruption in their ability to take-off?' – They would fly when it is open to the public.

'Combat ready when the public is on the aerodrome?' – Yes.

THE JUDGE: 'Do the public get on the runways on open day?'

AIR-COMMODORE MAGILL: ' Most certainly not.'

MR HUTCHINSON: ' It would not surprise you if 50,000 members of the public were on the aerodrome on open day?' – No, but they would be under proper control.

MR HUTCHINSON: ' When you say combat ready I suppose you mean what we used to call bombed-up . . . ?'

The Attorney-General interrupted: ' If my learned friend wants to find out armament the aircraft carry I shall have to go into camera.'

MR HUTCHINSON: ' I do not wish to use this trial in any shape or form to obtain information which is secret. On the question of whether the missiles carried on the aircraft are nuclear bombs or whether they are not I do not wish to go into camera and ask that particular question . . . I am perfectly content to conduct this case on the supposition they were.'

Mr. Hutchinson said that the Attorney in opening had indicated that he was calling Air-Commodore Magill to support his contention that the purpose of the accused was prejudicial to the safety and interest of the state.

' I am bound,' he said, ' to cross-examine this witness on whom the prosecution base their claim on the basis that he is not necessarily right about this.'

The Judge asked him if he insisted upon putting the question. If so the Court would have to go into camera.

Surely, said Mr. Hutchinson, it is not seriously suggested that it would be giving information to anyone for the Air-Commodore to say that planes in a state of combat readiness carried bombs – he had purposely avoided mentioning nuclear bombs. But the Judge insisted and the question was not pressed.

Shortly afterwards the jury were asked to leave the Court while the central question of what was admissible, and what was not admissible in evidence was discussed.

When the jury had left the Judge asked Mr Hutchinson to explain the line of defence he was putting forward. He had difficulty, he said, in understanding it.

Mr. Hutchinson explained that there were three basic points: Firstly he would seek to show that the defendants did not intend to prejudice the safety and interest of the state by their actions. Secondly, their beliefs were reasonable and well supported by evidence. Thirdly, their actions were not *in fact* prejudicial to the safety and interest of the state.

THE JUDGE: ' You are going to say it is far better if the aerodrome was not there or it was a playground?'

MR HUTCHINSON (after a pause): 'Yes, my lord, one might go as far as that.'

THE JUDGE: 'You are asking the jury to say that, nothwithstanding destroying the effect of the aerodrome, it was not prejudicial to the interest of the state?'

MR HUTCHINSON: 'I am saying that it was, in the view of the accused, beneficial. Their purpose was to do something beneficial to the state.'

The Attorney-General interrupted to say that a Communist spy could, on this basis, plead that it was in the interest of peace for countries behind the Iron Curtain to have certain information.

The legal argument, supported by citations from previous cases dating back to the case of Hampden and the Ship Money continued for the rest of the day and for most of the following morning. It was amazing how quickly the judge recalled the obscure cases referred to. He finally ruled that the purpose of the accused was relevant in going on to the airfield but not their motives or beliefs.

Furthermore any evidence which sought to challenge the defence system of the country could not be heard.

Evidence about the effects of nuclear explosions, the dangers of accidental war and anything of this kind was ruled out.

Next day the press described all this as a discussion of legal submissions and gave no details. Yet in this time the whole defence case had been ruled out of order.

The Attorney-General looked satisfied when the jury trooped back into their seats just before lunch on Wednesday morning. Air-Commodore Magill returned to the witness box.

Mr. Hutchinson asked a few questions but was ruled out of order. Then Pat Pottle began his cross-examination.

'Air-Commodore, if on December 9 you went to Wethersfield and demonstrators got into the base and sat or stood or lay down on the runways and there was an emergency call, what would you have done...'

THE JUDGE: 'What is the point of the question?'

PAT POTTLE: 'I am trying to establish whether the Air-Commodore with 5,000 troops and 850 policemen would have given orders to run over them by the aircraft taking off.'

ATTORNEY-GENERAL: 'He can't answer that. It is partly hypothetical and irrelevant.'

THE JUDGE: 'We can't have that.'

PAT POTTLE: 'Is there any official order you could not accept from the government...?'

THE JUDGE: (interrupting): 'He's an officer of the crown, Mr Pottle.'

PAT POTTLE: 'Is there any decision you cannot accept?'

AIR-COMMODORE MAGILL: 'It is my duty to carry out orders.'

PAT POTTLE: 'Would you press the button you know is going to annihilate millions of people?'

The Air-Commodore hesitated. People held their breath, but this time the Judge did not intervene.

'If the circumstances demanded it, I would.'

Pat Pottle continued: 'Have you read the summing up of the Judge at the Eichmann trial?'

The Judge asked: 'Where are we getting to?'

PAT POTTLE: 'What the Judge said in the summing-up at that trial. Perhaps I could read it.'

THE JUDGE: No, it has nothing to do with this case. I shall not admit it.

Pat Pottle paused and looked calmly through some papers: 'In the event of an emergency orders are going to be given not only to Wethersfield but to bases throughout this country. How much time are we going to have . . . . ?'

The Judge stopped him: 'I can't possibly allow that.'

PAT POTTLE: I was wondering. Does the Air-Commodore intend notifying everyone in this country . . . . ?

THE JUDGE: I can't allow that. If you want to ask these questions, I shall have to clear the court.

Pat Pottle then asked to be allowed to read an extract of a statement by Sir Winston Churchill in the House of Commons concerning NATO.

The Attorney-General said that that was irrelevant.

Pat Pottle went on to ask if it would be beneficial to the State and to the people of this country if bombers took off with nuclear weapons were this country to be attacked.

The Judge disallowed the question.

PAT POTTLE: Do you agree with the statement the Attorney-General made in his opening statement that those who are responsible for national security must be the sole judges of what national security requires?

The Judge directed the witness not to answer the question.

PAT POTTLE: Do you agree with the statement made by Mr Duncan Sandys in 1957 then Minister of Defence that bases could not defend people?

THE JUDGE: Don't answer him.

PAT POTTLE: When you said you would accept any order from the State, Adolph Eichmann's defence . . . .

The Judge interrupted: 'You cannot mention Eichmann in this case.'

Several more questions were ruled out of order by the Judge, including one referring to the Nuremberg trials.

Pat Pottle then referred to a Defence White paper. Would the Air-Commodore agree with this passage in it:

'It must be frankly recognised that there is at present no means of providing adequate protection for the people of this country against the consequences of an attack with nuclear weapons.'

Again the Judge told the witness not to comment. Pat Pottle complained that all the questions about whether the action contemplated was or was not prejudicial to the safety and interest of the State were being ruled out of order.

'We don't deny we planned to enter Wethersfield and tried to get others to do so. Only we say we done it for a purpose beneficial to the State.'

Pat Pottle's blunt questions, his down to earth speech with its touch of cockney, his occasional lapses of grammar were in brilliant contrast to the suave urbanity of the Court. Finally he said that since everything he asked and everything Mr Hutchinson asked was being ruled out of order he had no further questions.

After lunch Michael Randle went into the witness-box. He said he did not wish to take the oath and was allowed to affirm.

He said he had been secretary of the Committee until the end of last year. He agreed with other people to enter Wethersfield aerodrome and encouraged others to do so.

MR HUTCHINSON: Did you appreciate if, in fact, you entered that aerodrome you might well be committing some form of offence?

MICHAEL RANDLE: Yes, I was aware of this.

MR HUTCHINSON: If you had been charged with offences which in your view you had been guilty of, would you have pleaded guilty? – Yes.

Did you, in fact, agree to enter the R A F station for any purpose prejudicial to the safety or interest of the State? – No.

Did you ever incite other people to enter the aerodrome for a purpose prejudicial to the safety or interest of the State? . . . .

The Attorney-General rose and said that these were questions for the jury to determine.

The Judge said he would allow the question.

Michael Randle agreed that they had wished to enter for the purpose stated in a pamphlet of grounding all aircraft and demanding the reclamation of the base for civilian purposes.

'The further purpose was to bring home to people in this country that millions could be killed if nuclear weapons were used and therefore to try to prevent the massacre of millions of people.'

This aerodrome had been chosen because it was one of those which they felt might well be carrying nuclear weapons.

Mr Hutchinson: Sometimes the use of these weapons by aircraft is decribed as nuclear defence. In your view can there be such a thing as that? – I am quite certain there can be no such thing as nuclear defence, and I would quote Duncan Sandys, the Minister of Defence, whose White Paper in 1957 made it quite clear there could be no question of defending the people of this country but only defending nuclear bases.

Mr Hutchinson quoted from *Act or Perish,* and asked if he agreed with the pamphlet when it described nuclear weapons as weapons of mass extermination.

Michael Randle said that this was his view, and he thought recent statements by both Marshal Malinovsky and a US spokesman made it clear that in nuclear war there would be mass extermination.

Mr Hutchinson quoted a passage saying that experts had concluded present policy would be certain to bring disaster within a fairly short time and that governments did not wish the full facts to be known by ordinary people.

Michael Randle said that the Committee of 100 felt that people in Britain were not sufficiently aware of the facts and what they meant in human terms. These demonstrations would help to inform them and the campaign over the last few years had helped.

Mr Hutchinson further quoted: 'What is officially said about Civil Defence both here and in America is grossly misleading. The danger of fall-out is much greater than the authorities wish the population to believe.'

Michael Randle said he had not made a very great study of fall-out, but he thought the facts in the pamphlet were probably the case.

When Mr Hutchinson read further extracts the Attorney-General objected that they were not relevant.

The Judge: His view of whether nuclear war is a good or bad thing is quite immaterial.

Mr Hutchinson: Is your lordship ruling that this accused man is not entitled to give any evidence at all as to the purpose of his visit to Wethersfield?

The Judge: He has told us his purpose.

Michael Randle, asked by Mr Hutchinson if there were other facts he wished to bring home to the public, spoke of the danger of war by accident, misinterpretation of what was seen on a radar screen, or misinterpretation of orders.

The Judge: 'We cannot hear any more about nuclear armament. I must close it so far as the nuclear deterrent is concerned.'

In further replies Michael Randle said he had no desire to break the law for the sake of breaking it. He believed in democracy and the need to abide by the majority decision except in very exceptional circumstances.

The Judge asked if there was any justification for breaking the law.

MICHAEL RANDLE: An individual has to make a decision where millions of lives are concerned.

THE JUDGE: Does that mean you and other members of the Committee of 100? – Every individual must decide, and in that situation they have a right to make a decision. Every individual has to decide between the law and his own morality.

THE JUDGE: As far as I can see it means this, doesn't it? If you disagree with the law you break it? – Only in very exceptional circumstances. It does not mean if I disagree with the law I break it. It only means I break it in particular situations where it is against human rights.

Michael Randle said that use of nuclear weapons was always contrary to basic human rights. He could not see any situation where they would be justified against human beings. Civil disobedience did involve breaking the law, but it was integral that this should be by peaceful means.

In some situations, he felt, one was called upon not merely to disobey an order but to obstruct other people in carrying out what might be orders to them.

The object of the non-violent actions the Committee organised was to show an alternative way to the nuclear situation.

The object of the demonstrations was not simply to 'cause a nuisance' to the authorities, Michael Randle said.

'We want the authorities to have to make the decision whether they are going to take the sort of repressive measures against us that they are willing by implication to do in having nuclear weapons in the first instance.

'Having nuclear weapons presupposes a willingness to kill innocent people. We are saying to the authorities "If you want to do this you must first take repressive measures against us."

'Our purpose is not to obstruct justice as such but to make the authorities face up to the assumptions of their own policies. We are saying that if there are so many of us that the law courts are not sufficient to deal with us you might have to set up special camps – to shoot us if you like.

'This would demonstrate that these weapons are contrary to some of the democratic assumptions of our society.'

During the last twenty minutes of the day Michael Randle was cross-examined by the Attorney-General.

Michael Randle agreed that civil disobedience had been part of the Committee's purpose right from the beginning.

ATTORNEY-GENERAL: Right from the start it was a committee which joined together to engage in a campaign of law-breaking in a way it thought fit? – In a way we thought relevant and fit.

ATTORNEY-GENERAL: One reason for breaking the law was to draw attention to your views? – That is right. And to the facts.

The Attorney-General said: 'You may say they are facts, but I do not want to ask you about those kind of facts or your views. They may be what you thought were facts and what you thought were proper views, but I am not seeking to challenge your sincerity at all.'

In the last ten minutes the Attorney-General questioned Michael Randle about various statements that had been made to the effect that one of the objects of mass civil disobedience was to 'gum up the works' and make justice a farce. Was he still prepared to say under oath that this was one of the purposes?

The Court adjourned for the day. It was the first time the 'defendants' had been on the defensive.

Thursday started with a sharp exchange between Michael Randle and the Attorney-General.

ATTORNEY-GENERAL: Now, Randle . . . .

MICHAEL RANDLE: I am Mr Randle . . . Turning to the Judge he said: 'Can the Attorney-General please address me with courtesy?'

The cross examination continued. Answering further questions about obstructing the courts, Michael Randle said that the Committee certainly hoped for such large numbers that the courts would be unable to cope with the demonstrators. The Committee were also prepared to ask people to refuse to co-operate for the same reason. But the object was not to obstruct the normal work of the courts, but to make the authorities take special measures against demonstrators and face the logic of being prepared to commit genocide.

The Attorney-General then asked Michael Randle: 'You have said it is not necessary to be a pacifist to be a member of the Committee of 100. Are you a pacifist?'

Since the Attorney-General had from the beginning of the trial been insisting that the personal views and motives of the defendants were irrelevant, and the Judge had disallowed a question asking Inspector Stratton's views on nuclear weapons, Michael Randle queried whether his personal views about pacifism were relevant. The Attorney-General told him to answer the question. Michael Randle then asked the Judge if his personal views were relevant;

the Judge also told him to answer the question. Michael Randle then said: 'Yes, I am a pacifist.'

ATTORNEY-GENERAL: Why are you so reluctant to say whether you are a pacifist or not? – I say it is not relevant and I am asking the Judge to say it is not relevant.

ATTORNEY-GENERAL: Would you leave that to me?

Sir Reginald Manningham-Buller then went on to ask Michael Randle what salary he received from the Committee – the relevance of this particular question was not disclosed. Michael Randle replied that he and the other full time workers were all receiving between £7 and £9 a week – the Defence QC later referred to 'what my learned friend laughingly chooses to call a salary.'

Questioned about one of the documents which police had seized, Michael Randle said: 'I say quite openly that we are prepared to break the law where we think it is desirable.'

ATTORNEY-GENERAL: You arrogate to yourselves which laws should be broken by yourselves? – Yes. Where we feel the law is anti-social and going against the whole spirit of democracy.

You have told us you have been fined for obstructing the police. Do you think that law is anti-social? – I don't think that law is. I think the crime of genocide is. I think that people should go on to nuclear bases and should obstruct the police from removing them.

Questioned about the Wethersfield demonstration Michael Randle said he did not know for certain whether the aircraft there were carrying nuclear weapons.

ATTORNEY-GENERAL: So it was your plan to stop any aircraft leaving that base? – Exactly.

So Her Majesty's airfields can only be used by kind permission of the Committee of 100? – If we get specific assurance that they are not being used for atomic weapons we would not obstruct.

Your intention was to stop any plane leaving unless someone came and asked your kind permission? – That's about it.

It was then Pat Pottle's turn to cross-examine. He asked why the Committee consisted of 100 members and not just 10 or 15.

Michael Randle replied: 'So that every member would have collective responsibility and if any action was taken the Government would at least morally be pledged to take action against all of us.'

There was a ripple of laughter through the Court when, replying to a question by Pat Pottle about the exact role of the field secretary, Michael Randle referred to him as 'M' learned friend Mr Pottle.'

Mr Hutchinson now took up the cross-examination and questioned Michael Randle about his personal views. The Attorney-General objected, but Mr Hutchinson pointed out that as his learned friend had started this line of questioning by asking if Michael

Randle was a pacifist it was relevant for him to find out what had led the defendant to become a pacifist. The Judge allowed that this was reasonable.

When Mr Hutchinson asked about the moral issue, Michael Randle said it was morally indefensible to kill millions of people, and began to refer to the judgment in the Eichmann case. The Judge immediately interrupted: 'No, we can't have that.'

In all Michael Randle was in the witness-box for three and a half hours. Mr Hutchinson then told the Judge that in order to save the Court's time it was not his intention to call each of the accused to give evidence from the witness-box, but he understood they would each like to say something from the dock.

Trevor Hatton made a five-minute statement and the Judge wrote it down in his book in longhand:

'It is difficult to make the facts known to the ordinary man and woman such as the jury. Governments, and the Attorney-General represents the Government, are opposed to dissemination of knowledge which might cause dissatisfaction with their policy. I think it must be obvious from the conduct of this case that this is perfectly true. Your Lordship has ruled we are not allowed to call expert evidence which would show our purpose in going to Wethersfield was not prejudicial, but was, in fact, beneficial to the safety and interests of the State.'

Trevor Hatton added: 'I ignore the question of the safety or interests of the United States of America.'

He continued: 'Murder, we all agree, is a grave capital offence. The Attorney-General has prosecuted in such cases and you, my Lord, have tried such cases. Yet Air-Commodore Magill has said that in certain circumstances he would murder millions of people.'

Trevor Hatton delivered this statement in a quiet voice and with extreme politeness.

He added with the same mildness: 'I cannot understand why Air-Commodore Magill is not locked up. Is he not threatening genocide?'

He concluded: 'Any moment on this day or any future day while nuclear weapons exist and Governments threaten to use them we may all be wiped out instantaneously, or more unfortunately perhaps be left to linger on in a devastated world. Any possibility of justice will be destroyed and civilisation will be a shambles and justice a farce.'

Short statements were also made by Ian Dixon, Terry Chandler and Helen Allegranza.

Pat Pottle then began his defence: 'The Attorney-General in his opening speech said that the sole people who can say what is prejudicial to the State are the people that handle national security. I maintain the only people that can possibly say what is prejudicial or beneficial to the State are the people of this country. You are twelve representatives of the people of this country.

'Let us consider the evidence against the accused. Not one of the witnesses the Attorney-General has called has said our actions were prejudicial to the State. The only person in this trial who has so far said our actions were prejudicial to the State is the Attorney-General himself.

'Even the expert witness, Air-Commodore Magill, did not make this statement.'

Pat Pottle said he had hoped to bring evidence of the destructive power of nuclear bombs.

The Judge interrupted and told him: 'You can't bring in that – I have ruled that that is inadmissible.'

Pat Pottle then asked the Judge: 'Can I call evidence regarding the hazards of nuclear fall-out after nuclear bombs had been used?'

The Judge replied: 'No. In these matters I have ruled they are inadmissible.'

Pat Pottle said they were morally justified in breaking the law: 'If I didn't break the law I would be a criminal. If I don't break the law I am condoning the Government's decision to have these bases which can annihilate millions of people.'

He spoke of the Russian atomic tests: 'I can remember the British and American Governments two months ago condemning the Russians for exploding the 65 megaton bomb and I joined in that protest. We were arrested for sitting down outside the Russian Embassy.

'Yet the Government can say to us "It is in the interest of the State." We are saying that whoever tests bombs it is not in the interest of any State.'

Pat Pottle's first witness was Archbishop T. D. Roberts, former Roman Catholic Archbishop of Bombay, now living in Mount Street, London.

Asked if he was a pacifist, he replied: 'In the sense that Christ said "Every peacemaker is blessed".' During the war he had been a Padre to the forces in India and had been decorated.

Pat Pottle asked the Archbishop if he thought nuclear weapons were wrong on moral grounds, but the Judge ruled the question out of order, saying that the Court was not interested in morality.

Pat Pottle, continuing his questions to Archbishop Roberts, was about to ask him about Christian Martyrs when the Judge interrupted with: 'We are not concerned with Christian Martyrs, we are simply concerned with whether you have committed a breach of the Official Secrets Act and nothing else.'

Pat Pottle then asked him: 'Which, in your view, is the highest law, the moral law or ....'

Again the Judge interrupted him and said: 'You can't have that' – 'Then I have no further questions for the Archbishop.'

The next witness was Dr John Fergus King, who said he was a fighter pilot in the RAF between 1940 and 1946 and was awarded the DFC. Last summer he attended an open day at Wethersfield air base and in his opinion there were about 50,000 people there. They were all milling about and picnicking generally. Had there been an emergency it would have been extremely difficult to have got any planes off the ground.

If 50,000 had gone into the base on December 9 they would have done exactly the same thing as the 50,000 people did on the open day.

Pat Pottle asked him: 'Did you approve of the decision to immobilise the base?' – 'Yes.'

'Do you consider the decision of the Committee to do this was in the interests of the State?' – 'Yes.'

The next witness was Vanessa Redgrave, who was asked by Pat Pottle: 'Did you conspire with other people and incite other people to go to Wethersfield base on December 9?'

As she replied 'Yes, I did,' the Judge tried to stop her and told her: 'Before you answer that it is my duty to warn you that you are not bound to answer any question that you think might tend to incriminate you.'

Pat Pottle then put the same question to her and again she replied: 'Yes, I did.'

Pat Pottle continued: 'And was the purpose in your view in the interests of the State?'

The Attorney-General rose. He and the Judge said simultaneously: 'We can't have that.'

Pat Pottle then asked her: 'Was it your intention to incite other people to go to the base and to block and immobilise it?' – 'Yes.'

'In fact, did you hope in doing this you would stop nuclear bombs from being carried out from the American base in planes?' – 'Yes.'

'It was your intention to stop these planes from taking off?' – 'Yes.'

'You assumed the planes had nuclear weapons on board' – 'Yes.'

'You went there to try and stop planes from taking off and you believed they had nuclear weapons on them and you knew they could lead to the deaths of millions of people?'

The Judge, before Vanessa Redgrave could answer, told her: 'You must not answer that.'

Pat Pottle asked her: 'Do you believe that nuclear weapons mean, if they were used, total annihilation....'

The Judge (to Vanessa Redgrave): 'Don't answer this.'

Pat Pottle continued: 'Do you believe in England possessing nuclear weapons and if they are ever used that it means total annihilation of the English people....'

The Judge again interrupted and said: 'I rule that out. It is inadmissible.'

The next witness was Gene Sharpe, who is now at Oxford doing research into resistance aginst totalitarian régimes. Citing his qualifications as an 'expert' on non-violent action, Gene Sharpe said he had been awarded his MA in sociology at Ohio State University for a thesis on non-violence, had done research at the Institute of Social Research at Oslo University, and had been assistant editor of *Peace News*.

The Judge refused to allow Pat Pottle to question him on the ethics of non-violent civil disobedience and said: 'I am afraid we can't turn this court into a college for non-violence.'

The next expert witness for the defence was Sir Robert Alexander Watson-Watt, the inventor of radar, now living in New York, who had flown from the USA to attend the trial. A formidable list of Sir Robert's qualifications emerged, including the fact that he had held posts in meteorology, radio and radar in several Ministries, including the Air Ministry, and had been deputy chairman of the Radio Board of the War Cabinet from 1943 to 1945. Pat Pottle elicited the fact that in the past Air-Commodore Magill had been one of Sir Robert Watson-Watt's subordinates.

However, Sir Robert was not allowed to say much more than the other expert witnesses when Pat Pottle began to question him.

Pat Pottle protested to the Judge, saying Sir Robert was the greatest expert on radar in the world and now found he could not give evidence on radar systems.

He was then allowed to ask Sir Robert if it was possible for the radar systems now being used in this country and America to distinguish between a missile and a flock of geese.

SIR ROBERT: It is perfectly possible for modern radar to distinguish between a flock of geese, an aircraft, a missile, or the rising moon.

Sir Robert said that in the early days of radar this kind of definition had not been possible. He said he had observed human error and was aware of its very serious consequences.

Pat Pottle then asked Sir Robert if he felt that nuclear bases in the United Kingdom were beneficial and in the interests and security of the State.

The Judge refused to allow the witness to answer and also refused to allow him to answer a question about whether there was a strong possibility of an accident in the radar systems of many countries.

Pat Pottle asked Sir Robert: 'In the event of there being an accident millions of people are going to die. I do not think we can just pass this off as saying that all machines sometimes have an accident because if they do we have all had it.'

The Judge intervened and told Sir Robert: 'You cannot answer that.'

Pat Pottle asked: 'Is it only human error that is going to create an accident with these bombs or is it that they are not technically right to distinguish between all forms of natural phenomena?'

The Judge did not wait for Pat Pottle to finish his question, but directed Sir Robert: 'Don't answer that.'

Pat Pottle went on: 'Do you regard not only the base at Wethersfield but nuclear bases in this country as beneficial or prejudicial to the safety of the population?'

THE JUDGE: 'You can't answer that.'

PAT POTTLE: 'Do you regard these bases as a danger to the survival of mankind?'

THE JUDGE: 'You can't answer that.'

Pat Pottle then observed to the Judge: 'All the questions I was hoping Sir Robert could answer and all the questions which Sir Robert has flown from America to answer I am unable to ask, and so I have no further questions to ask Sir Robert.'

The Attorney-General said he had no questions to ask Sir Robert.

On Friday the hearing was postponed because Pat Pottle had suddenly collapsed. Medical evidence was given to certify that he could not appear in Court that day.

The Attorney-General expressed concern that Pat Pottle should have proper medical treatment, and Mr Justice Havers remarked that there was an excellent hospital at Brixton. (One wonders whether this judgment was based on first-hand evidence.) Mr Hutchinson pointed out that it would greatly inconvenience the defence if consultations had to be carried on at Brixton prison, and Pat Pottle himself remarked that he felt the atmosphere at home would be more restful mentally and more conducive to his recovery.

He was granted bail. The hearing was adjourned till Monday.

When the trial was resumed on Monday Pat Pottle thanked the

Court for allowing him to go home on Friday when he was not feeling well.

He called into the witness-box to give evidence on his behalf Professor Linus Pauling, who said he lived at Pasadena, California, and was a professor of chemistry at the California Institute of Technology, and was a citizen of the United States of America.

He was a foreign member of the Royal Society, a member of the Royal Institute, and in 1954 was awarded the Nobel Prize for Chemistry. He also had the Presidential Medal of Merit which was the highest award a citizen of the United States could receive.

Answering Pat Pottle, Professor Pauling said that he supported the Committee of 100.

PAT POTTLE: Why?

The Attorney-General rose to object to the question, and the Judge told Pat Pottle: 'I think this is out.'

PAT POTTLE: You have sent telegrams and made speeches in support... Again the Attorney-General rose to object and the Judge told Pottle: 'He has said he supports it.'

Prof. Pauling said that he was at Trafalgar Square on September 17 but not at Wethersfield last December, but he supported the Wethersfield demonstration and had discussed a demonstration of this type of civil disobedience in other countries.

'Have you yourself supported any civil disobedience, say, in America?' – 'I have not taken part in civil disobedience myself, but I am a supporter.'

Pat Pottle then began to read a quotation to him and the Attorney-General stopped him, saying 'This cannot be relevant.'

The Judge ruled that the question was irrelevant, saying that he had given Pat Pottle great latitude because he was not represented. 'Learned counsel would have obeyed my rules and so must you,' he said.

Pat Pottle attempted to question Professor Pauling further about his qualifications.

THE JUDGE: It isn't much good getting his qualifications as an expert if he isn't allowed to give the facts. I can't allow any expert evidence on nuclear weapons. I have ruled that.

Pat Pottle attempted to ask a question about Governments trying to suppress the facts.

THE JUDGE: Quite immaterial.

Pat Pottle then tried to ask a question about Civil Defence and the Judge ruled: 'You can't put any questions about that.'

Questioned further, Prof. Pauling said that until recently his scientific work was the whole of his life. Then the Judge interrupted saying 'This can't be relevant to the jury.'

PAT POTTLE: Why is it that you have spent so much time speaking and writing and in this case coming specially to this country for this trial?

THE JUDGE: I can't allow that.

Pat Pottle asked Prof. Pauling's views on disarmament which was again not allowed.

PAT POTTLE: As a scientist, as a chemist with full knowledge of the facts which we are not permitted to have, do you consider that a nuclear war....

THE JUDGE: I have told you you can't ask these kind of questions.

Pat Pottle told Prof. Pauling: 'I must apologise for your journey over here and I thank you for all the help you have been permitted to give.'

Bertrand Russell, who was the next witness, affirmed saying he had a conscientious objection to taking the oath. He refused a chair and said he would stand.

He told the Court that he had won the Order of Merit in 1949, was made a Fellow of the Royal Society in 1908, was a Fellow of Trinity College, Cambridge, and had won the Nobel Prize for Literature in 1950.

PAT POTTLE: A lot of evidence has been brought into this case on the history of the Committee of 100 and why the Committee feels justified in committing civil disobedience.

THE JUDGE: Just listen to me. If any question is asked which you think will incriminate you you are entitled not to answer.

Pat Pottle then asked Bertrand Russell his purpose in forming the Committee of 100.

BERTRAND RUSSELL: My purpose was to try and avoid the extermination of the people of this country and of many millions elsewhere.

PAT POTTLE: Did you agree with the Committee's decision to go to Wethersfield?

THE JUDGE: Bear in mind what I told you.

BERTRAND RUSSELL: Yes, I did.

PAT POTTLE: Can you explain your purpose in wanting to go to Wethersfield? – It seemed that this country and a lot of the major countries of East and West were in dire peril and it was our duty to make it known.

PAT POTTLE: Is one of the purposes of committing civil disobedience to get the facts known about the dangers? – Yes, in my opinion.

PAT POTTLE: On September 12 you were sent to prison because you would not deny your political beliefs....

THE JUDGE: That is quite irrelevant.

PAT POTTLE: I have a statement made by Lord Russell....

THE JUDGE: It is inadmissible.

Mr Hutchinson then rose and pointed out that in the transcript of the third day of the trial the Attorney-General in cross-examining Randle had asked him about his objects and trying to attract public support.

ATTORNEY-GENERAL: This can't be relevant.

THE JUDGE: You can't ask any more questions on that.

Bertrand Russell agreed that he and the Rev. Michael Scott were authors of the leaflet *Act or Perish*.

PAT POTTLE: Have you thought it funny these past few weeks that the six people in the dock gave out this leaflet and are in the dock for doing so and yet you who wrote it are not accused?

THE JUDGE: Don't answer.

PAT POTTLE: Did you conspire and incite people to go to the Wethersfield Base?

The Judge then repeated his warning about incriminating questions and Bertrand Russell had difficulty in hearing.

PAT POTTLE: The Judge is saying you need not answer if you think it would be incriminating.

Bertrand Russell asked the Judge: 'Have I not the right to incriminate myself?'

THE JUDGE: My duty is to warn you, the same as for witnesses who might not know. You are perfectly entitled to incriminate yourself.

BERTRAND RUSSELL: Well, I do.

PAT POTTLE: Did you conspire and incite people to block Wethersfield base? – Yes.

Do you feel you are just as responsible as the people in the dock? – I do.

PAT POTTLE: You have taken a decision to commit civil disobedience. Can you elaborate on why you have taken this decision?

THE JUDGE: No he can't.

After attempting to put a further question which the Judge refused Pat Pottle then told the Court: 'I have no further questions. I would like to thank Lord Russell and say he is an inspiration to us all.'

The Attorney-General then rose to cross-examine Bertrand Russell, and asked: 'Were you at the meeting of the working group which planned this operation?' – 'No.'

'Randle has told us right from its inception the Committee of 100 intended to embark on a plan of civil disobedience?' – 'Yes, that is right.'

'And that means breaking the law?' – 'That is also right.'

'What was your object in agreeing to the demonstration at Wethersfield?' – 'To get the facts known.'

'That was the whole object of your agreeing to the demonstration?' – 'In my case yes; no doubt different people have different objects.'

Pat Pottle re-examined Bertrand Russell, asking him: 'You said you did not attend the meeting that decided to have the demonstration at Wethersfield? But were you kept informed day by day by telephone as to what was going on, and did you approve of the decisions that were made?' – 'Yes, I was kept constantly informed

Bertrand Russell added: 'I had every opportunity of expressing disagreement, but I felt none.'

Pat Pottle's last question was: 'You feel as responsible as all members of the Committee of 100?' – 'At least as much, and as President perhaps rather more.'

All evidence in the case had been heard by Monday, February 19, when the Prosecution and the Defence made their closing speeches. Pat Pottle, who was defending himself, spoke first for 25 minutes. He spoke with assurance and conviction in what one of his hearers described as one of the best speeches ever made on behalf of the Committee of 100.

He pointed out that the vast majority of the social advantages obtained in the past century had been through civil disobedience – for example, the right of women to vote and of men to join a trade union.

'Could any of us condemn them for doing it? Can any of us condemn what is going on in Georgia where Negroes today are sitting in cafés and restaurants?

'It seems to me this country is always saying how marvellous it is what coloured people are doing in Georgia and Africa and South Africa and that civil disobedience is a good thing so long as it does not happen in England, when it is a bad thing.'

The Committee had organised demonstrations against nuclear weapons and nuclear war. The real object was to try and make the ordinary man and woman in this country aware of the danger of war. Our planet is covered with nuclear bases such as Wethersfield.

'I could not call witnesses as to opinion or as to the justification of committing civil disobedience. I could not call witnesses as to the moral question of possessing nuclear weapons. You may ask yourselves what the defence is left with as to its purpose for these actions.

'If you feel we were not allowed to bring any evidence as to our purpose there is only one verdict you can possibly bring in, and that is Not Guilty.'

Pat Pottle drew the jury's attention to the fact that the only man in the Court who said the purpose of the accused was prejudicial to the safety of the State was the Attorney-General, who had called no witnesses to substantiate this.

Mr Jeremy Hutchinson, Q.C., spoke for the other five defendants. In fact, he frequently spoke for all six, though he referred to the excellent speech made by Pat Pottle in his defence.

In a forceful speech which concentrated less on the political defence and emphasised the legal aspects of the trial, Mr Hutchinson seized on the Attorney-General's claim that the jury should only be concerned with facts and not with beliefs or opinions, and referring to the Attorney-General's long cross-examination of Michael Randle about his pacifist opinions, asked:

'Why ask the question, why go into it? Why ask the questions about civil disobedience? Why ask if the only question for you, the jury, to decide is did they mean to stop the planes and was it prejudicial?

'Civil disobedience has a great deal to do with it if their aims and motives are relevant. How on earth, in all common sense – and for goodness sake let's apply some – how can you consider the purpose of anybody without looking at their views on which the purpose is founded?'

He pointed out to the jury that it was easy to say 'These people are a nuisance.' 'Of course they are a nuisance to the authorities and a great many people.

'They are an irritant to the authorities and you may think they are an irritant to the consciences of a great many people as well.'

Mr Hutchinson then referred to his own examination of Michael Randle, in which he had asked 'Did you intend to do anything prejudicial to the interests and safety of the State?'

'Immediately the Attorney-General objected and said that was a question for the jury to decide. Where, indeed, have we got if a man is asked in the number one Court at the Central Criminal Court whether he committed a crime and is not allowed to answer because it is a question for the jury?

'One begins to wonder whose case it is. Is it Air Commodore Magill's, is it Detective-Inspector Stratton's, or is it the United States Air Force's?'

In summing up for the prosecution the Attorney-General referred with outrage to Michael Randle's evidence. Never, he said, in the history of the Old Bailey had he known such effrontery.

Sir Reginald Manningham-Buller emphasised that 'this is not a prosecution by the Government.' He also stressed that the prosecution was not brought because of the views of the accused but because they had 'deliberately broken the criminal law of the land.'

He explained to the jury that whilst they were out of the Court the Judge had ruled that the beliefs and opinions of the defendants were inadmissible, and this was why the witnesses called for the Defence had often not been allowed to answer any questions.

In dealing with the fact that only six members of the Committee of 100 were in the dock the Attorney-General commented 'You may think others may count themselves fortunate whether on account of age, or for any other reason, that they are not in the dock.'

In a peroration he said that the Committee put themselves above the law, and asked the jury to consider what would happen if other bodies acted in the same way. 'If they succeeded it would be the end of the rule of law and would lead to the end of democracy, to anarchy, and to a dictatorship.'

Finally the Judge in summing up said: 'You have heard the evidence of Air-Commodore Magill, the director of operations for the Air Ministry. You may think holding that position qualifies him as a competent person to express a view on operational aspects.

'He said that there were planes at that air base which had a vital part to play in the defence of this country and it was an essential part of the defence of this country.

'If you accept that evidence, do you think the defences of the country would be impaired or weakened because those aircraft had a vital part to play in the defences and would either be impeded or prevented from taking off?

'If you are satisfied that this would be or was likely to be the result if the plan of the accused was carried out, would the result be prejudicial to the safety of the State?'

Mr Justice Havers then embarked on a somewhat obscure discourse on the likelihood of the next war being nuclear or non-nuclear. 'We do not know if war ever comes again in which this country is involved whether our potential enemy will have nuclear weapons or not. Nobody knows.'

He also disposed rapidly of the relevance of the defendants' commitment to non-violence. Referring to violent and non-violent action he said: 'If they succeeded in holding up aircraft, blocking and immobilising that air base, the effect would be precisely the same whether they had used violence or non-violence.'

Before passing sentence the Judge, Mr Justice Havers, stated that he was prepared to be very lenient if the accused would admit the error of their ways and would undertake to give up illegal demonstrations. They were all asked in turn whether they would give this promise, and they all refused.

The Judge then made a final speech before passing sentence, in which he said the accused stood guilty of committing serious offences against the country, and that it was not for want of trying, but owing to the good sense of the majority of people in this country that they had not succeeded in their intention of immobilising the Wethersfield air base on December 9. He felt obliged to impose a sentence that would deter others from taking the same action – eighteen months for the men and twelve months for Helen Allegranza.

Official England is no doubt pleased with its work. It is up to radical England to make that pleasure as short lived as possible.

Bertrand Russell

MY VIEW OF THE COLD WAR

Bertrand Russell wrote this article to explain his attitude towards Communism and the Soviet Union and to answer those 'Cold War propagandists' he accused of distorting his views. It was published in the April 1964 issue of an American peace movement magazine, 'Minority of One'.

One of the more reprehensible characteristics of our time is the power to colour the judgment of whole populations which has come about through the concentration of political power and the advent of mass media of communication. In a sense, people do not behave very differently from the way their ancestors did in pre-agricultural and tribal society. Taboo operates very powerfully in the social and personal activity of most human beings. What is new is the uniformity of attitude which can be so quickly induced in people, even when the attitudes jeopardize their obvious well-being.

In all major wars the opponents have considered each other desperately wicked and capable of actions reprehensible beyond the understanding of the noble defenders of the right. In this century, for example, the English-speaking peoples of Europe and America have fought two World Wars. In the first World War, the Germans were enemies, the Japanese tacit allies and the Russians were enemies and allies in the same war. In the Second World War, the Germans were again enemies, the Japanese were enemies and the Russians were enemies and allies in the same war but in reverse order.

Before 1945 was out the Russians were enemies, the Germans and Japanese were allies and the populations of the respective countries were learning to hate their former friends and applaud their recent enemies. It is hardly possible that the reasons for these shifts in attitudes were soundly arrived at. It is because the crass struggles for power which have characterized relations between nation states have now been granted a sanctity through the mass media that was not so easy to achieve at any time between the religious wars and the present, that murderous passions are so fickle.

The war to end wars was waged, so Americans told us, to make the world safe for democracy. I do not know that Czarist Russia and Imperial Japan were ideal spokesmen for that political abstraction, but not many noticed this and what mattered were the flag and national glory.

The Russian Revolution was an event welcomed at first by all who loathed the tyrannical backwardness of feudal Russia. Many, however, were slow to see the tyrannical possibilities in a one-party state and a messianic dogma. When I pointed out these dangers in my book *The Practice and Theory of Bolshevism,* I was condemned as alarmist and those who applauded did not do so because they hated tyranny but because they feared socialism. Similarly, today the most vociferous opponents of Soviet Communism are not troubled by the cruel tyrannies which can be found throughout Europe, Latin America and the Near and Far East, many of which are part of the 'free world.' This moral and political astigmatism is caused by the power to shape people's minds by colouring the information provided them and by bullying people into accepting a distorted view of any national rival.

I have been engaged in a prolonged public effort to make people realise the appalling danger of the Cold War. I have been so engaged because the attitudes I have described earlier in this article are leading to the agonising death of our species and I consider this a pity. The death of mankind strikes me as a more important issue than the differences which powerful men exaggerate for the purpose of furthering national rivalries.

My approach since the advent of massive nuclear arming has been to point out that neither side could be justified in imposing the risk of annihilation of humanity. My object has been to convince people of the folly of conflict, to remind them that often in the past the very governments and populations now locked in deadly struggle were joined in it against other opponents.

I have sought to point out that the weapons systems and the warning systems together provide a death sentence for man and that miscalculation, if nothing else, will cause the final calamity. In particular, I have tried to overcome in people the vast sense of helplessness they feel in the face of the overwhelming danger of nuclear war. I have not encountered much indifference in people to the prospect of annihilation. There is immense ignorance but not true indifference. Rather, I have seen that most people feel utterly paralysed by the vast impersonal machinery of war and state power, of massive institutional life and of the relentless pace of world events. People no longer feel any ability to change things. As individuals they feel that their desires have no bearing on events and that they are without any serious means of making their desires count in the world outside themselves. This social crippling of individual human beings in our time has contributed greatly to the acceptance of events and to the embrace of pernicious national myths fostered by those in power.

If, thinks the ordinary man, everyone has nuclear bombs and everyone threatens the other with them; if our planet is covered by rocket bases which can discharge their deadly arsenals in an instant; if great and powerful governments insist upon this state of affairs and declare it necessary; if only traitors or sympathisers with the enemy oppose such things, then how can I do anything about it?

When people accept passively a situation they feel to be wrong or dangerous, they sacrifice their personal responsibility and to an extent which cannot easily be gauged, their self-respect. They become first helpless observers as if at a theatrical event, then embarrassed apologists and finally slightly cynical advocates of malicious things and condemners of all who have not travelled this damaging path.

The psychology of mass acquiescence in the day to day danger of global death which I have tried to outline very summarily affects professional people every bit as much as ordinary working people. Professional people who impinge on public opinion are further subjected to the pressure of those who are in power and to the pressure of the orthodoxy of the moment. When these pressures combine to make them willing advocates of things they know to be shockingly evil, they become enslaved to their weakness, no longer capable of recognising the truth, of cherishing independence of judgment or of desiring to examine alternative points of view.

My own experience of these developments has fallen in line with their general effect. When I advocate conciliation and oppose the policies of nuclear threat and preparation, I am put down as an agent of the 'enemy.' It is carefully fostered in the United States that I apologise for Soviet policy. This is done, of course, because I oppose American policy. It is not noticed that I have spoken, written and publicly demonstrated against those Soviet actions which I consider wrong, for over forty years. When I condemn Soviet tests, the Ulbricht régime or the Soviet treatment of Jews this is explained away as a 'departure.' When I condemn the policy of the United States in Cuba and Vietnam, this is dismissed as Soviet propaganda.

Any who read my books can see that I condemn nuclear policy and support steps away from this policy without respect to who takes them. But public opinion is not shaped by books. It is created by the ununiformed policemen of the great powers who write for the mass media and reflect the dangerous orthodoxies of the men who wield power.

I shall end this article with a very clear example of what I mean. Whenever I read American accounts of the reasons for the failure to agree with the Russians on disarmament, it is said that the cause lies in the refusal of the Russians to agree to inspection or controls. This is almost universally believed in America. It is continuously repeated in the American press and by commentators such as James Reston. It is stated quite untruly that Russia rejects any inspection until the whole process of disarmament is complete.

The actual Soviet position is this: If the West agrees to the *principle* of general disarmament, the Russians will permit internationally recruited inspection teams to be placed in every country *before any measure of disarmament begins.* After the agreement to the principle of general disarmament, the Russians offer to allow:

1) Thousands of United Nations inspectors on Soviet soil before any reduction of armaments starts;
2) Inspectors to control *on the spot* the disbanding of 60% of Russian manpower, *all* (100%) of the means of delivery of missiles, and *all* other carriers.

I have tried in vain to point out to the peoples of the West that their governments are not telling the truth about the Soviet position on disarmament. When I do so, I am said to be apologising for Soviet policy.

At the time of the Cuban crisis I praised Khrushchev warmly because he preferred giving way to a nuclear war. I condemned Kennedy for preferring the risk of a nuclear war to giving way. I wish above all an end to the risk of mass murder. I favour agreement and I consider no issue to be important enough to sacrifice agreement to nuclear conflict. I cannot sacrifice my own responsibility to warn and to speak the truth, to a fear of being accused of being pro-Soviet when I praise Soviet conciliation, or of being thought a Western dupe when I condemn Soviet intransigence. It is horrible shrinking from dispassionate consideration of the merits of a stated view because of its authors, and it is the fear of an unpleasant truth, which prevent us from behaving decently. This state of mind, no less than this state of affairs, is driving mankind to death. And we are responsible.

Ray Gosling

NO SUCH ZONE

Ray Gosling one of the most articulate of young writers expressing the 'Teenage Thing' from within wrote these reactions to the Cuba crisis for 'Peace News', *February 22 1963.*

Mr Christopher Isherwood is a fine, sensitive writer; a socialist, committed, conscious and concerned with the world and us – yet in 1938 when it seemed certain that there was going to be a war, what was his reaction?

> '... I had supper with B, at the flat. Since I was there last B has bought a big mirror and hung it in the bedroom. We drank whisky, and then had sex in front of it... But there was something cruel and tragic and desperate about the way we made love; as though we were fighting naked to the death. There was a sort of rage in both of us – perhaps simply rage that we are trapped here in September 1938 – which we vented on each other. It wasn't innocent fun, like the old times in Germany – and yet, just because it wasn't – it was fiercely exciting. We satisfied each other absolutely, without the smallest sentiment, like a pair of animals.
>
> *(Down there on a visit)*

Those empty, liberal men of the 1930s; those impotent middle-class radicals who couldn't make any protest. Faced with the prospect of their country plunging headlong into a second world war, they welshed and ran away in a flood of self-pity.

But, naturally, since 1938 everything has changed so much.

> All the Allied raids on Germany during the six years of World War II killed about 500,000 people.
> Two small A-bombs dropped on Japan in August 1945 killed at least 100,000 people.
> Early A-bomb (Hiroshima) 20,000 tons of TNT.
> Latest H-bomb (1961) 50,000,000 tons of TNT.
>
> *(Black Paper)*

So much has happened. CND. New Left.

On Leicester Square the fallen leaves lifted lazily from the ground. The display outside the cinema read – ' The day history held its breath – THE LONGEST DAY!! ' Already there was a queue. At the BBC, in the depths of Bush House canteen, a woman from Lively Arts in green-grey suede said to me – ' But wouldn't it really be just terrible if it did happen? Odds on you'd end on a word like " blast " . . .', and there was a roar of laughter from This is Britain (The Authentic Voice).

> ' It seemed to us that nothing useful could be achieved by ordinary people within 24 hours to prevent this event. We therefore decided to go as swiftly as possible to a place where we might conceivably survive a nuclear war – the west coast of Ireland.'
>
> *Pat Arrowsmith and Wendy Butlin, letter to ' Peace News ', November 2.*

I had arrived in London around mid-day, and it was all very exciting. I felt caught up in the life of a capital where everything was going so fast, like a 33⅓ playing at 78 counter-revolutions. Little vans in purple and silver-grey aluminium screeched around corners wearing headboards, freshly stuck, proclaiming ' Doom. Megadeath. Cuba.' The faces of people in the street seemed all lit up; snatching up new editions to read the headline before the horses. God, it must have been marvellous in the war. Now I know – the comradeship, everyone being so kind, so friendly; the keeping of a stiff upper lip with a sour joke. The people of London had risen to the occasion, marvellously: stunned, surprised and paralysed as they are whenever there has been a sudden fall of snow, or a strike on the Underground.

> ' I went down to the American Embassy this evening. But the sense of futility was so great that I felt I was demonstrating more out of force of habit than because anything was being achieved.'
>
> *(Richard Boston: A diary of eight days, ' Peace News ', November 2).*

Arrived at C's in time for *Panorama*. There were four of us, sitting in front of the screen – glued to an emotion-charged, round voice – Please remain seated. Hold your breath for an all human humourless horror. The fire curtain is about to rise on this play where each of us has a part to play as statistic (insignificant, dispensable, or disposable). And it came from less than a 2s. tube ride away, through the ether and down the grey tube to evaporate just before it arrived at the eye. This is a joke: a terrifying set-up joke: an epic as glorious as The Coronation of Her Majesty: a part of series Drama '62 – so supersonic and so thrilling, that like 'one mega-death' it is beyond all our understanding. We watched in silence. I let myself out. Go home and wait.

> 'No one shouted "Hands off Cuba". Numbed and dazed, the people of Bristol stood together in the centre of their city and waited to die.'
>
> *(Sanity, December)*

Walked away from C's, slowly down Shaftesbury Avenue towards Piccadilly Circus for the bus. The streets were almost deserted apart from the newspaper fellas, making good on the same headline of 'any minute now.' I queued for the bus. In front of me, silent and serious, were a group of Canadian sailors when from behind comes this man, all greasy raincoat and he starts off a raughting about the good the Canadians did in the last war when the Americans let us down, and how in this war we'd all stand together once again. And looking across at me were the red dots of the *Sunday Times* hoarding – 'The Hidden Face of British Communism by Aidan Crawley' – 'I'll pay the bus fares. I'll pay for you,' he says to the Canadians.

The bus arrives, and up the stairs we all go. The bus starts, but there still on the pavement stands the greasy-mac man, pressing money into the conductor's hand, smelling too sober and shouting after the bus – 'They'll keep us free. They're not Yankees. They'll not let us down.' – Round and down Haymarket, the conductor coming up the stairs with 'fares please' and the Canadians getting out their money, and the conductor saying 'It's all right, the man paid for you,' and people chuckling when suddenly this big bang – and silence on the upper deck. I looked out of the window and there on the street are two nippers letting off their bangers and squibs and laughing away. No one laughed on the upper deck. Still quiet. Along Pall Mall. No raughting. No smiles. A silence of small stones.

> 'Waited all evening. Sat in the pub in complete despair. When someone spoke, which was rare, you didn't know if they would get to the end of the sentence.'
>
> *(Richard Boston: A diary of the eight days).*

By Victoria coach station one paper seller was saying to the other – 'We can sell these last few to them that come off the coaches. They won't know' – and the last papers still said – any minute now.

It was half past ten as the men lifted their bundles into the station, nearly four hours stale.

Got into the flat and went upstairs to join the after-dinner party. Talk rolled over large brandies and small cigars, and I kept looking at my watch and wanting to say – can we switch on the radio for the news? – but talk went on and on: liberal, intelligent: about the UN, and England and Israel as if years were ahead – but what of those ships, what if . . . and as the minutes ticked up to midnight I was still too small and frightened of the power of intelligent men to say – the news, shall we hear the news? – then at last people rose to say – I have to be up early. I really must go now. Alone I turned on the radio, turned to AFN and after Squires and Clooney and Anka and Riddle came the newscast brought to you by the wires of AP, UP, and . . . .

Russell had sent a telegram. The ships hadn't met. The Russians seemed to be turning back. Went to bed, impotent, exhausted, passive, gelded, an Isherwood of the 60s.

In the morning there was heavy rain. At the coach station bookstand the woman was carrying on: 'Oh, it had me worried. It really had me worried. It was just like the war it was, yesterday.'

And didn't we love it, all of us. Like cannibals we love to eat ourselves, obsessed with suicide: and wasn't it fun, because we were all running to the cliff's edge like sheep to the slaughter, and over the edge.

And we loved it. We were at the centre of things; our military blood, our love of fighting and crisis, and war and order – for we know our place –we were playing a part we knew very well – Kings and Pawns. We weren't having to think for ourselves. There was no point. There are only two parts we are happy at – the leader and the led; élite and statistic.

And the aluminium vans were screaming around on the wet tarmac – 'India latest!' – and the newsboard read – 'PM on Cuba' – and the morning papers were thick with it – at last their language fitted the facts; at last there was order and drama, good and bad, black and white.

The epic was over.

By the afternoon the papers were hunting for a repeat performance; their sabre-rattling clichés were fitting around INDIA – CHINA – THE YELLOW PERIL.

I walked past Foyles, and the little woman in black, faithful as ever, held out – 'Peace News. Pacifist paper. 'Peace News'. – pathos – protest.

I gave a letter to the postman,
He put it in his sack.
But by early next morning
He brought my letter back.
    She wrote upon it,
Return to Sender.
Address unknown.
No such number.
No such zone.

(Elvis Presley)

Spike Milligan

LANCE-CORPORAL MILLIGAN JOINS THE MINISTRY OF DEFENCE

'Tribune', *December 23, 1960*

By paying a search fee of five shillings, and suffering the customary insults of civil servants, I was allowed to see the marriage registers of Somerset House.

After three hours among the Ms, I discovered what I had hoped, there was a marriage of my great-great-grandfather, Timothy Brian Boin Milligan to Miss Jill *Macmillan.*

I was in! Related to the P.M.! For several hours, wearing a hand-made Clan Macmillan centrally-heated kilt, I stood in a queue of Macmillans outside Number 10.

Finally, about dividend time, I was shown into the great man.

'Do sit down' he said, indicating the floor, 'be with you in a jiff,' he said and proceeded to put on several Eton, two Harrow and three Lords Taverners' ties. 'Got to keep in with 'em' he yawned, 'it's the only way these days.' A G.P.O. Democratic monopoly phone rang.

'Hello, Prime Minister of England here ... No no, not yet, we'll wait for the Fords hoo ha to die down first before the next one. Bye Henry, oh, Henry? ... tell them to lay off any take-over bids of publishing firms eh? There's a good boy. Bye now.

He turned to me, 'So, you're one-tenth Macmillan?'

'Yes I am sir.'

'We can still be friends eh? ha ha, suppose you want a job?'

I nodded, 'Look, we're a bit short of speeches for the Minister of Defence, he's been slipping lately, I mean, making statements that have no double entendre. If you can write one that well, one that well, er well you know, one that er....'

'I *think* I know *exactly* what you mean sir.'

'Good boy, you've got the right idea ... now, do you own a pencil?'

'Outright.'

'Splendid, here's a White Paper, fill it in.'

He shook me by the hand, gave me a travel voucher and a Macmillans' Christmas Catalogue of 'Suitable Book Presents for Members of All Parties. Free postage to our clients in USSR.'

At dawn, after the Christmas recess, Mr. Harold Watkinson, Minister of Defence, read from my typewritten paper.

HANSARD REPORT OF DEFENCE SPEECH – 1961

Mr. Speaker, Honorable Members . . . (here there were cries of p——off, from Opposition Back Benchers). This morning, I have pleasure in giving the Government's estimate for next year's Defence Budget 1961-62. Eight hundred and forty-five million, two hundred and sixty-three hundred thousand, three hundred and forty-two pounds, eight shilling and eightpence three farthings. Postage four and a penny.

Extras and taxi fares – nine million, three hundred and forty-nine thousand, six hundred and spon. This puts our Defence Budget up by four hundred million on last year (applause from Tory benches. At this stage Mr. Crapington Plitt, Liberal M.P. for a tree in Berkshire, intervened).

Mr. Crapington Plitt: Does this mean we are in fact safer?

Min. of Defence: Of course, we are obviously four million pounds safer, less super tax of course.

Mr. Crapington Plitt: Do the Russians know this?

Min. of Defence: No . . . no . . . but we will be sending them our military bank statement and *that* ought to give them food for thought. Ha ha.

(Light applause, tea, cakes and scratching from Tory benches break out).

Mr. Feet, M.P.: What plans are being made for our Forces at Christmas?

Min. of Defence: All is in hand, the time of goodwill will be observed, with its message of Christmas hope for mankind.

Mr. Feet: What form will this take?

Min. of Defence: All intercontinental ballistic missiles will be festooned with fairy lights, and nuclear warheads hung with seasonal holly.

Mr. Squtts (M.P. for a lunatic asylum in Alleppo): But these missiles you speak of, they're not British! . . . .

Min. of Defence: Ah no! but . . . *but!!* . . . their presence here puts Britain in a position of power, this great deterrent that has given us peace on earth and goodwill to all men for so long, is now on British soil . . . I . . . .

(Cries of ' American bum ', and a cry of ' Let's have a little more libel ' from Strangers' Gallery. A man called Randolph is asked to leave).

Min. of Defence: I admit that these bases have been built by Americans, manned by Americans, and that Americans alone have the power to decide if and when the missiles are fired, but, nevertheless and as much thereto, the men who sweep the missiles' platforms and stand guard in the pouring rain are BRITISH!!!

(Ecstatic applause, from the Tory benches, singing of National Anthem breaks out. Speaker restores order by distributing non-voting G.M.C. shares).

Mr. Feet (Labour): In the event of an H-bomb dropping on Aldershot, what would be the rôle of our troops?

Min. of Defence: The prime job of our Army is to defend England, but, should an H-bomb fall on Aldershot, the troops, would be transported to safety, to say Scotland, and stand ready to defend England.

Mr. MacNutts (Labour): Supposin' that they drop an H-bomb on Scotland . . . Ireland, Wales and, well, the lot?

Min. of Defence: The Army would be flown to the safety of Canada, and stand ready to defend England from there.

Mr. Feet: Are you saying that it is possible for H-bombs to destroy England?

Min. of Defence: Never! There'll always be an England.

Mr. Feet: Never mind England – what about the English people?

Min. of Defence: Oh *them?*

(Here the Labour Backbenchers took to song with – 'There'll always be a Radioactive England.' Fighting Foot and Mouth and Kingsley Martin broke out, etc., etc.)

John Osborne

A LETTER TO MY FELLOW COUNTRMEN

'Tribune', *August 18, 1961*

This is a letter of hate. It is for you, my countrymen. I mean those men of my country who have defiled it. The men with manic fingers leading the sightless, feeble, betrayed body of my country to its death. You are its murderers, and there's little left in my own brain but the thoughts of murder for you.

I cannot even address you as I began as 'Dear', for that word alone would sin against my hatred. And this, my hatred for you, and those who tolerate you, is about all I have left and all the petty dignity my death may keep.

No, this is not the highly paid 'anger' or the 'rhetoric' you like to smile at (you've tried to mangle my language, too). You'll not pour pennies into my coffin for this; you are MY object. I am not yours. You are my vessel, you are MY hatred. That is my final identity. True, it will no doubt die with me in a short time and by your unceasing effort.

But perhaps it could be preserved, somewhere, in the dead world that you have prepared for us, perhaps the tiny, unbared spark of my human hatred might kindle, just for the briefest moment in time, the life you lost for us.

I fear death, I dread it daily. I cling wretchedly to life, as I have always done. I fear death, but I cannot hate it as I hate you. It is only you I hate, and those who let you live, function and prosper.

My hatred for you is almost the only constant satisfaction you have left me. My favourite fantasy is four minutes or so non-commercial viewing as you fry in your democratically elected hot seats in Westminster, preferably with your condoning democratic constituents.

There is murder in my brain, and I carry a knife in my heart for every one of you. Macmillan, and you, Gaitskell, you particularly. I wish we could hang you all out, with your dirty washing, on your damned Oder-Neisse Line, and those seven out of ten Americans too. I would willingly watch you all die for the West, if only I could keep my own miniscule portion of it, you could all go ahead and die for Berlin, for Democracy, to keep out the red hordes or whatever you like.

You have instructed me in my hatred for thirty years. You have perfected it, and made it the blunt, obsolete instrument it is now. I only hope it will keep me going. I think it will. I think it may sustain me in the last few months.

Till then, damn you, England. You're rotting now, and quite soon you'll disappear. My hate will outrun you yet, if only for a few seconds. I wish it could be eternal.

I write this from another country, with murder in my brain and a knife carried in my heart for every one of you. I am not alone. If WE had just the ultimate decency and courage, we would strike at you – now, before you blaspheme against the world in our name. There is nothing I should not give for your blood on my head.

But all I can offer you is my hatred. You will be untouched by that, for you are untouchable. Untouchable, unteachable, impregnable.

If you were offered the heart of Jesus Christ, your Lord and your Saviour – though not mine, alas – you'd sniff at it like sour offal. For this is the Kind of Men you are.

Believe me,

In sincere and utter hatred,

Your Fellow Countryman,

JOHN OSBORNE

Valbonne, France

C. Wright Mills

A PAGAN SERMON TO THE CHRISTIAN CLERGY

The late Professor C. Wright Mills was a Professor of Sociology at Columbia University, New York, and author of several books including The Power Elite *and* The Causes of World War III. *His* Pagan Sermon to the Christian Clergy *was widely distributed in the United States in 1960, where it caused intense controversy. It was first published in Britain in* ' Peace News ', *December 16 1960.*

To say that war has become total is to say that the reach of modern weaponry now makes every soul on earth a quite possible victim of sudden hell. It is to say that weapons have become absolute, and every calculation from on high now includes a military calculation.

It is to say that the decision makers of every nation, in particular those of the United States, are now possessed by the crackpot metaphysics of militarism. But more than that: it is to say that the morality of war now dominates the curious spiritual life of the fortunate peoples of Christendom.

World War III is already so total that most of its causes are accepted as ' necessity '; most of its meaning as ' realism.' In our world ' necessity ' and ' realism ' have become ways to hide lack of moral imagination. In the cold war of politicians and journalists, intellectuals and generals, businessmen and preachers it is above all else moral imagination that is most obviously lacking. One reason for this lack, I am going to argue, is what must surely be called the *moral default of the Christians.*

The ethos of war is now the ethos of virtually all public thought and sensibility. But I must limit this article to the fact of moral insensibility in the Western world and to the religious failure that supports it.

By moral insensibility I refer to the mute acceptance – or even the unawareness – of moral atrocity. I mean the lack of indignation when confronted with moral horror. I mean the turning of this atrocity and this horror into morally approved conventions of feeling. I mean, in short, the incapacity for *moral* reaction to event and character, to high decision and the drift of human circumstance.

Such moral insensibility has its roots in World War I; it became full-blown during World War II. The ' saturation bombing ' of that war was indiscriminate bombing of civilians on a mass scale; the atomic bombing of the peoples of Hiroshima and Nagasaki was an act committed without warning and without ultimatum. By the time of Korea, the strategy of obliteration had become totally accepted as part of our moral universe.

The pivotal decision, made by the United States and by the Soviet Union, is the monstrous one, as Lewis Mumford has put it, of trying ' to solve the problem of absolute power, presented by nuclear weapons, by concentrating their national resources upon instruments of genocide.'

The spokesman of each side say they know that war is obsolete as a means of any policy save mutual annihilation, yet they search for peace by military means and in doing so they succeed in accumulating ever new perils. Moreover, they have obscured this fact by their dogmatic adherence to violence as the only way of doing away with violence.

There has not before been an arms race of this sort – a scientific arms race dominated by the strategy of obliteration. And at every turn of this hideous competition, each side becomes more edgy, and the chance becomes greater that accidents of character or of technology will trigger the sudden hell.

The key moral fact about this situation is the virtual absence within ourselves of absolute opposition to these assumptions of our ruling élites, to their strategy, and to the policies by which they are carrying it out. And the key public result is the absence of any truly debated alternatives. In some part the absence both of opposition and of alternatives rests upon, or at least is supported by, the fact of moral insensibility.

Between catastrophic event and everyday interest there is a vast moral gulf. Who in North America experienced, as human beings, World War II? Men fought; women waited; both worked. About the war they all said the same kind of things. Nobody rebelled, nobody knew public grief. In the emotional economy there was efficiency without purpose.

It was a curiously unreal business. A sort of numbness seemed to prohibit any real awareness of what was happening. It was without dream and so without nightmare, and if there were anger and fear and hatred – and there were – still no mainsprings of feeling and conviction and compassion were let loose in despair or furor; no human complaint was focused rebelliously upon the political and moral meanings of the universal brutality.

People sat in the movies between production shifts watching with aloofness and even visible indifference, as children were ' saturation bombed ' in the narrow cellars of European cities. Man had become an object; and in so far as those for whom he was an object felt about the spectacle at all, they felt powerless, in the grip of larger forces, having no part in those affairs that lay beyond their immediate areas of daily demand and gratification.

It was a time of moral somnambulance. And worst of all, from the religious point of view, the people of this continent were often brightly hopeful – while what used to be called the deepest convictions were as fluid as water.

It is as if the ear had become a sensitive soundtrack, the eye a precision camera, experience an exactly-timed collaboration between microphone and lens. And in this expanded world of mechanically vivified communications, the capacity for experience is alienated, and the individual becomes the spectator of everything but the human witness of nothing.

In all the emotional and spiritual realms of life, facts now outrun sensibility, and these facts, emptied of their human meanings, are readily gotten used to. There is no more human shock in official man; there is no more sense of moral issue in his unofficial follower. There is only the unopposed supremacy of technique for impersonal calculated, wholesale murder.

This lack of response I am trying to sum up by the altogether inadequate phrase 'moral insensibility,' and I am suggesting that *the level of moral sensibility, as part of public and private life, has in our time sunk below human sight.*

Religion today is part of this sorry moral condition; to understand the crucial decisions of our pivotal times it is not necessary to consider religious institutions or personnel or doctrine. Neither preachers nor laity matter; what they do and what they say can be readily agreed with, and safely ignored. I am aware that there are exceptions, but the average output is correctly heard as a parade of worn-out phrases. In the West, religion has become a subordinate part of the overdeveloped society.

If there is one safe prediction about religion in this society, it would seem to be that if tomorrow official spokesmen were to proclaim XYZ-ism, next week 90 per cent of religious declaration would be XYZ-ist. At least in their conforming rhetoric, religious spokesmen would reveal that the new doctrine did not violate those of the church.

As a social and as a personal force, religion has become a dependent variable. It does not originate; it reacts. It does not denounce; it adapts. It does not set forth new models of conduct and sensibility; it imitates. Its rhetoric is without deep appeal; the worship it organises is without piety.

It has become less a revitalisation of the spirit in permanent tension with the world than a respectable distraction from the sourness of life. In a quite direct sense, religion has generally become part of the false consciousness of the world and of the self.

Among the cheerful robots of the mass society, not human virtue but human shortcomings, attractively packaged, lead to popularity and success. They are men and women without publicly relevant consciousness, without awareness of shocking human evil, and their religion is the religion of good cheer and glad tidings. That it is a religion without dreary religious content is less important than that it is socially brisk and that it is not spiritually unsettling. It is a getting chummy with God, as a means to quite secular good feelings.

With such religion, ours is indeed a world in which the idea of God is dead. But what is important is that this fact itself is of no felt consequence. Men and women, in brief, are religiously indifferent; they find no religious meanings in their lives and in their world.

The verbal Christian belief in the sanctity of human life has not of course been affected by the impersonal barbarism of twentieth-century war. But this belief does not itself enter decisively into the plans now being readied for World War III.

A savage politician once asked how many divisions the Pope had – and it was a relevant question. No one need ask how many chaplains any army that wants them has. The answer is: as many as the generals and their other satraps feel the need of. Religion has become a willing spiritual means and a psychiatric aide of the nation-state.

Total war must indeed be difficult for the Christian conscience to confront, but the current Christian way out makes it easy; war is defended morally and Christians easily fall into line – as they are led to justify it – in each nation in terms of 'Christian faith' itself. Men of religious congregations do evil; ministers of God make them feel good about doing it. Rather than guide them in the moral cultivation of their conscience, ministers, with moral nimbleness, blunt that conscience, covering it up with peace of mind.

The moral death of religion in North America is inherent neither in religion nor specifically in Christianity. At times this religion has been insurgent; at other times, complacent; and it has been characterised by repeated revivals. Just now it is neither revolutionary nor reactionary, and it makes no real effort to revive itself in order to examine great public issues and the troubles of individuals from a fresh religious perspective. It does not count in the big political balance of life and death.

This is not surprising. In their struggle for success religious institutions have come into competition with two great contemporary forces; amusement and politics. Each of these has been winning over religion; and when religion has seemingly won over them, it has failed as religion.

The most obvious competition is with the world of industrialised entertainment. Competing with these mass means of distraction, churches have themselves become minor institutions among the mass media of communications. They have imitated and borrowed the strident techniques of the insistent publicity machines, and in terms of the pitch-man (with both the hard and the soft sell), they have quite thoroughly banalised the teachings, and indeed the very image, of Christ.

I do not believe that anything recognisably Christian can be put over in this way. I suggest that this religious malarkey *diseducates* congregations; that it kills off any real influence religious leaders might have. Even if the crowds come, they come only for the show, and if it is the nature of crowds to come, it is also their nature soon to go away. And in all truth, are not the television Christians in reality armchair atheists? In value and in reality they live without the God they profess; despite 10,000,000 Bibles sold each year in the United States alone, they are religiously illiterate.

'If Christ had been put on television to preach the Sermon on the Mount,' Malcolm Muggeridge has recently remarked, 'viewers would either have switched on to another channel, or contented themselves with remarking that the speaker had an interesting face. Christ might have become a television personality, but there would have been no Christianity.'

If you, as Christian ministers, accept the entertainment terms of success, you cannot succeed. The very means of your 'success' make for your failure as witnesses, for you must appeal to such diverse moral appetites that your message will necessarily be generalised to the point of moral emptiness. If you do not specify and confront real issues, what you say will surely obscure them. If you do not alarm anyone morally, you will yourself remain morally asleep. If you do not *embody* controversy, what you say will inevitably be an acceptance of the drift to the coming hell.

And in all this you will continue well the characteristic history of Christianity, for the Christian record *is* rather clear: from the time of Constantine to the time of global radiation and the unintercept-ible missile, Christians have killed Christians and been blessed for doing so by other Christians.

Politics, like religion, has of course also come into competition with and been deeply influenced by the world of entertainment and its means of attraction and distraction. But the realities of politics and of economics are nowadays very difficult to ignore; they just won't lie down, for they are part of the insistent military lie that now dominates official civilised endeavour.

Religion cannot compete with this political peril. What vision of hell compares with the realities we have and do now confront? And the point is that ministers of God are not foremost among those few men who would define and expose the morality of the political decisions and lack of decisions that lie back of these morally atrocious events and preparations. For a church whose congregation contains all political views and which is out for statistical success feels it must prosperously balance 'above' politics – *which means that it serves whatever moral default the affairs of mankind reveal.*

As a mass medium, religion has become a religiously ineffective part of the show that fills up certain time slots in the weekly routine of cheerful robots. The minister goes his curious way, bringing glad tidings into each and every home.

Believe me, I do not wish to be rude, but I am among those pagans who take declarations seriously, and so I must ask you, as declared Christians certain questions:

What does it mean to preach? Does it not mean first of all, to be religiously conscious? I do not see how you can preach unless as a man you are the opposite to the religiously indifferent. To be religiously conscious, I suppose, is to find some sort of religious meaning in one's own insecurities and desires, to know oneself as a creature in some kind of relation with God which increases your hope that your expectations and prayers and actions will come off. I must ask: for you, today, what is that religious meaning?

To preach, secondly, means to serve as a moral conscience, and to articulate that conscience. I do not see how you can do that by joining the publicity fraternity and the weekend crusaders. You cannot do it by 'staying out of politics.' I think there is only one way in which you can compete as religious men with religious effect: you must be yourself in such a way that your views emanate unmistakably from you as a moral centre. From that centre of yourself you must speak.

So I must ask: why do you not make of yourself the pivot, and of your congregation the forum, of a public that is morally led and that is morally standing up? The Christian ethic cannot be incorporated without compromise; it can live only in a series of individuals who are capable of morally incorporating themselves.

Do not these times demand a little Puritan defiance? Do not they demand the realisation of how close hell is to being a sudden and violent reality of man's world today?

Should not those who still have access to the peoples of Christendom stand up and denounce with all the righteousness and pity and anger and charity and love and humility their faith may place at their command the political and the militarist assumptions now followed by the leaders of the nations of Christendom? Should they not denounce the pseudo-religiosity of men of high office who would steal religious phrases to decorate crackpot policies and immoral lack of policies?

Should they not refuse to allow immorality to find support in religion? Should they not refuse to repeat the official, un-Christian slogans of dull diplomats who do not believe in negotiation, who mouth slogans which are at most ineffective masks for lack of policy? Should they not realise that the positive moral meaning of what is called ' neutralism ' lies in the resolve that the fate of mankind shall not be determined by the idiotically-conducted rivalry of the United States and the Soviet Union?

I do not wish to be politically dogmatic, but merely brief, and, as you gentlemen surely have recognised, I am religiously illiterate and unfeeling. But truly I do not see how you can claim to be Christians and yet not speak out totally and dogmatically against the preparations and testing now under way for World War III.

As I read it, Christian doctrine in contact with the realities of today cannot lead to any other position. It cannot condone the murder of millions of people by clean-cut young men flying intricate machinery over Euro-Asia, zeroed in on cities full of human beings – young men who two years before were begging the fathers of your congregations for the use of the family car for a Saturday night date.

There is no necessity for more military emphasis on missiles. There is no need for more ' science ' in education; it is not ' realism ' to spend more money on arms. *Necessity and need and realism are the desperate slogans of the morally crippled.* The necessity is for moral imagination. The need is for political new beginnings. Realism means to stop at once and if need be unilaterally all preparations for World War III. There is no other realism, no other necessity, no other need.

You will not find in moral principles the solution to the problems of war, but without moral principles men are neither motivated nor directed to solve them. But nowadays we pagans see that Christian morals are more often used as moral cloaks of expedient interests than ways of morally uncloaking such interests.

War is not today inevitable; it is, immediately, the result of nationalist definitions of world reality, of dogmatic reliance upon the military as the major or even the only means of solving the explosive problems of this epoch of despair and of terror. And because this is now so, to lift up and to make knowledgeable the level of moral sensibility is the strategic task of those who would be at peace.

Your role in the making of peace is less the debating of short-run and immediate policies than the confrontation of the whole attitude toward war and the teaching of new views of it by using them in criticism of current policies and decisions. And in the end, I believe the decisive test of Christianity lies in your witness of the refusal by individuals and by groups to engage in war. Pacifism, I believe, is the test of your Christianity – and of you. *At the very least, it ought to be THE debate within Christendom.*

The brotherhood of man is now less a goal than an obvious condition of biological survival. Before the world is made safe again for American capitalism or Soviet Communism or anything else, it had better be made safe for human life.

But you may say: 'Don't let's get the church into politics.' If you do say that, you are saying: 'Don't let's get the church into the world; let's be another distraction from reality.' This world *is* political. Politics, understood for what it really is today, has to do with the decisions men make which determine how they shall live and how they shall die. They are not living very well, and they are not going to die very well, either.

Politics is now the locale of morality; it is the locale both of evil and of good. If you do not get the church into the moral issues of politics, you cannot confront evil and you cannot work for good. You will be a subordinate amusement and a political satrap of whatever is going. You will be the great Christian joke.

Men and ideas, the will and the spirit are now being tested, perhaps in all truth for the final time; and in this testing so far you Christians are standing in default. The key sign of this is the fact of your general lack of effective opposition, of your participation in the fact of moral insensibility. That, of course, is a world fact about publics and masses and élites, but it is all the more grievous among Christians, if only because of the expectations that they have aroused about themselves.

Yet who among you has come out clearly on the issues of internecine war and the real problems of peace? Who among you is considering what it means for Christians to kill men and women and children in ever more efficient and impersonal ways? Who among you uses his own religious imagination to envision another kind of basis for policies governing how men should treat with one another? Who among you, claiming even vague contact with what Christians call 'The Holy Spirit,' is calling upon it to redeem the day because you know the times are evil?

If you are not today concerned with this – the moral condition of those in your spiritual care – then, gentlemen, what is your concern? As a pagan who is waiting for your answer, I merely say: you claim to be Christians. And I ask: What does that mean as a biographical and as a public fact?

In moral affairs you are supposed to be among the first of men. No moral affair today compares with the morality of warfare and the preparation for it, for in these preparations men usurp – as you might say – the prerogatives of God. By sitting down and by keeping quiet, by all too often echoing the claptrap of the higher immorality that now passes for political leadership – you are helping to enfeeble further in this time of cruel troubles the ideals of your Founder.

Christianity is part of the moral defeat of man today. Perhaps it is no longer important enough to be considered a cause of it; perhaps it is only among the passive doctrines of the spectators of man's moral defeat.

I hope you do not demand of *me* gospels and answers and programmes. According to your belief, my kind of man – secular, prideful, agnostic and all the rest of it – is among the damned. I'm on my own; you've got your God. It is up to you to proclaim gospel to declare justice, to apply your love of man – the sons of God, all of them, you say – meaningfully, each and every day, to the affairs and troubles of men. *It is up to you to find answers that are rooted in ultimate moral decision and to say them out so that they are compelling.*

I hope your Christian conscience is neither at ease nor at attention, because if it is I must conclude that it is a curiously expedient and ineffective apparatus. I hope you do not believe that in what you do and in how you live you are denouncing evil, because if you do, then I must conclude that you know nothing of evil and so nothing of good. I hope you do not imagine yourselves to be the bearers of compassion, because if you do you cannot yet know that today compassion without bitterness and terror is mere girlish sentiment, not worthy of any full-grown man.

I hope you do not speak from the moral centre of yourself, because if you do, then in the dark nights of your soul, in fear and in trembling, you must be cruelly aware of your moral peril in this time of total war, and – given what you, a Christian, say and believe – I, a pagan, pity you.

Michael Scott

A CHRISTIAN APOLOGY FOR NON-VIOLENT RESISTANCE

The Rev. Michael Scott, honorary director of the Africa Bureau, former RAF pilot and co-founder with Bertrand Russell of the Committee of 100, wrote the following for ' Peace News ', *March 31 1961.*

Someone has unkindly defined the Church of England as the Conservative Party at prayer. It cannot be denied that among many conservatively minded people the Christian religion is a great preserver of law and order if not its ultimate sanction. Any suggestion of its being subversive they would think rather blasphemous.

Some years ago when I was in Nyasaland, at the time when the Central African Federation was being imposed on the people of Nyasaland and the chiefs and people were trying to organise passive resistance, I remember being denounced over the radio in Nyasaland for telling the chiefs I thought there was nothing incompatible between non-violent civil disobedience and the Christian religion. ' The powers that be are ordained of God,' said the Bishop. And ' Submit yourselves unto every ordinance of man for the Lord's sake.'

More recently I have read of other Christian leaders whom I had thought to be sympathetic towards non-violent resistance saying much the same. Some leaders of CND have objected to civil disobedience in Britain on the grounds that it is inexpedient where democratic rights exist. Even in South-West Africa, where democratic rights do not exist and there is a friendly Bishop who is a member of the Fellowship of Reconciliation, he is reported in the *Windhoek Advertiser* of December 8, 1960, as saying that ' Enforced apartheid was recognised as a social sin by all major Christian bodies, with one exception, throughout the world.' He felt he could never withhold witness to the sin of imposed apartheid, whatever the possible consequence. God loved the whole world. ' The Church points out that God loves not only individuals who respond to Him, and not only the Church, but all human society, that Christ is interested in the whole life of the world. There is no separate and isolated compartment of life called " religion ". The voice of the

Church must be heard on social as well as other evils, and in this respect imposed apartheid and imposed separate development must be condemned.'

The Bishop declared his deep respect for lawful authority, the *Windhoek Advertiser* report added, continuing:

'The Government of South Africa and South-West Africa was obviously making a supreme effort to carry out its determined policies at great cost and great courage. Whatever our personal views of their actions, we had to respect whatever government was in power, according to the teaching of Jesus and Paul.

'The challenging of an imposed apartheid on the one hand and the respecting of the Government on the other might seem inconsistent, unless they considered the basic Christian method of correcting wrong – that evil can only be conquered by facing it in love, accepting it and absorbing it. This was the only acceptable Christian method. Such actions as boycotts were, in the light of this belief, fundamentally unacceptable. The Bishop quoted instances from the Scriptures to support this doctrine of non-resistance – as opposed to what is generally referred to as passive resistance.'

While it is true that Christ's resistance to evil was not expressed in specifically political action, yet he clearly foresaw and even courted the consequences of his own positive actions. Humanly speaking, he could have gone on preaching his gospel of 'peace on earth amongst men of good will' until it was time for him to retire, but he 'set his face to go up to Jerusalem.' And it was notably at this point that his disciples began to hold back in fear and even to begin an argument about the Kingdom coming in another world and who would be the greatest in it.

It only needed one positive action challenging a long established abuse to rouse the establishment and start the process which destroyed Him. This action He took against a custom whereby traders within the Temple precincts exploited the poor who came to pay their tributes and by the animal sacrifices required of them.

It was immediately after this first challenge to a strongly entrenched vested interest from which the Church itself benefited that the machinery of propaganda was set in motion. And it was not long before the insidious whispering campaign about His claims had reached such dimensions that the very crowds which had hailed Him as the Deliverer, 'Hail to the Son of David,' were shouting 'Crucify Him! Crucify Him! Not this man but Barabbas' (the terrorist).

As the great drama of Christ's passion moves towards its climax it is evident that a great spiritual conflict is being fought out. Paradoxically it appears as a conflict between freedom and necessity.

There is the compulsion of law, custom and tradition backed by force; and opposed to it there is the strength of a free spirit making an affirmation of faith in the indestructible power of truth whatever the consequences to Himself.

The strength of non-violent resistance grows in intensity from the Sermon on the Mount to the Mount of Golgotha. The inner secret and unique genius of Jesus is to be found in this mounting intensification of non-violence. From peaceful persuasion by word of mouth it grows into positive non-violent action challenging the forces of hatred and violence by methods and means against which the argument of brute force is not merely powerless but self-defeating.

In this sense Christian understanding and forgiveness are not just 'non-resistance,' nor merely an easy-going tolerance of evil of which the antithesis is conceived to be strong moral condemnation, but the more powerful form of passive resistance which is the only means by which evil can be overcome, and the conflict between good and evil resolved. This is the form of non-violent resistance to oppression and other social evils of which the world stands desperatly in need at every level of life. But it is precisely here that the inner secret of Christ's religion has been corrupted and distorted throughout history into varying forms of intolerance and mutually exclusive systems of salvation and arrogant nationalisms.

Yet the inner logic has been there for all to see all through the ages. The promise of fulfilment of the hopes of all mankind is in the birth of Bethlehem of peace on earth amongst men of good will. The new teaching attracted the crowds all round Lake Galilee because it struck a new note of hope in the ultimate omnipotence of love as the solvent of injustice and oppression. (If a Roman soldier compels you to go a mile carrying his luggage go with him two. If you are struck turn the other cheek. If you don't like the Roman system of currency being imposed on you give it back to Caesar to whom it belongs. Later he was charged with instigating non-payment of taxes).

The logical implications of this non-resistance were only applied in their fullest intensity at His trial on charges of blasphemy and treason. He did not deny these charges but refused to plead, although the judge was clearly on his side. His non-co-operation made inevitable the final act in this divine human tragedy. There, on the Cross, the human spirit attains its highest possible achievement in even finding excuses for human ignorance and folly, but above all in the prayer for forgiveness of his torturers made in the last throes of death: 'Father, forgive them for they don't know what they are doing.'

We may not ourselves as preachers or politicians be able to rise to the same height of divine folly and wisdom in dealing with human ignorance and cruelty that are revealed in this timeless story of the divine human interaction from Bethlehem to Calvary. But at least let us not diminish its power, the depth and height of its dimensions, or its urgent relevance for our own time by calling it undemocratic or dismissing it as moral blackmail. To do so would be to rob the Christian religion of its heart and the innermost meaning of it – to take away the crown of thorns and replace it with a bowler hat.

Yet that is what has happened. The Cross has become the symbol of respectability instead of the conflict with evil and injustice that it was to the early Christians. And now it needs to be rediscovered in the struggle against the menace of nuclear war. For even in an advanced democratic state such as ours, social progress is made often by small minority groups who have remained true to their principles in spite of majority opposition and who are prepared to stand by them both by parliamentary and extra-parliamentary action.

But now it is sought to make the Cross a symbol of Established Religion and a sanction of law and order. At all levels of society people are busy washing their hands of responsibility and sit upon a judgment seat evading the truth for themselves with the metaphysical question 'What is Truth?'

They try to turn this religion into an 'ideology against Communism' (Moral Rearmament), or a sanction for Christian Nationalism, Imperialism, apartheid and a chaotic multiplicity of conflicting systems of salvation. And they, the monopolists of Grace and Truth, point fingers of scorn at one of the greatest philosophers of our time sitting on a pavement outside the Ministry of Defence in a mild variation of Christ's challenge to the Law of Imperial Rome and the Ecclesiastical Establishment of his day.

But while they claim to be building up the defences of Christian civilisation by amassing more and more deterrents the danger looms larger of a nuclear crucifixion of humanity through the inability of any one nation to make the great venture of faith in God and man which perhaps only a nation that really believes in a creative purpose on earth could make. It may be that to Britain is given an opportunity to lead a break-through of mankind's historical dilemma since the very magnitude of the powers of destruction show them to be self-defeating and a new approach to be so urgently necessary if humanity is to survive.

Some lines of A. E. Housman were quoted in meditation on the

Sahara Protest team as we sat in the hot dry dust on the frontier of the (then French) Upper Volta:

If in that Syrian garden ages slain
You sleep and know not you are dead in vain
Nor even in dreams behold how dark and bright
Ascends in smoke and fire by day and night,
The hate you died to quench and could be fan –
Sleep well, and see no morning, son of man.
But if, the grave rent and the stone rolled by,
At the right hand of majesty on high
You sit, and sitting so remember yet
Your tears, your agony and bloody sweat,
Your cross and passion and the life you gave,
Bow hither out of heaven and see and save.

Herbert Butterfield

HUMAN NATURE AND THE DOMINION OF FEAR

Professor Herbert Butterfield, Master of Peterhouse and Professor of Modern History in Cambridge, delivered this lecture at the American University, Washington DC, under the auspices of the School of International Service and the Wesley Theological Seminary. It was subsequently included in a collection of lectures, published under the title International Conflict in the Twentieth Century. *The following slightly abridged version was published as a pamphlet, with the author's permission, by the Christian Campaign for Nuclear Disarmament.*

Fear is a thing which is extraordinarily vivid while we are in its grip; but once it is over it leaves little trace of itself in our consciousness. It is one of the experiences that we can never properly remember – one, also which since we may be ashamed of it we may have reason for not wishing to remember.

Because it is so hard for us to recapture the feeling in our imagination, we can be thoroughly nonparticipating where there is question of a fear that is not our own. If another person is the victim of it, we may fail – or it may never occur to us to try – to apprehend either the thing in itself or the range of its possible consequences. It would seem that we are not always easily convinced of the existence of fear in other people, especially when the other people are political rivals or potential enemies. At any rate historians are not easily convinced when they deal at a later time with former enemies of their country. Above all, if the thing which the other party dreaded is a danger that never materialised, it becomes easy to be sceptical about the genuineness of the fear itself. When the historian cannot escape recording the terror that Napoleon inspired, or the German dread of Russia at one time and another, or the apprehension of a people in the face of imminent attack, he may produce a factual statement that gives little impression of the force and the effect of the emotion actually experienced. Sometimes he is jolted into a realisation of his deficiency as he finds himself confronted by an event and sees that the rest of his picture provides only an inadequate context for it. It turns out that there was some standing factor in the story – a terrible feeling of thunder in the atmosphere – which he had imperfectly apprehended or merely failed to keep in mind.

The student of history needs to consider this question, therefore. Some aspects of the past – and these perhaps the ones more related to men's minds and moods – are particularly difficult to recapture. The atrocities of our own day, for example, are naturally more vivid to us than those of a century ago. The world tends to judge a present-day revolution merely by its atrocities and an ancient one much more by its ideals and purposes. This is partly because the sufferings and terrors of a former generation are more easily overlooked. We need to possess something of the art of the dramatist in order to enter into the sensations of other people – to recover, for example, the 'feel' of some terror that once possessed a nation or a ministry. And it must not be said that we ought to leave our imagination out of our history, for the minds of men, and even the mood of society, may have their part in accounting for human conduct. Even when the student of the past is really bent on analysis, he must recapture the fear, and the attendant high pressure which so greatly affect the actions of men and the policy of governments. Yet the historical imagination is never so defective as when it has to deal with the apprehension and insecurity of frightened people. It is a point to remember, therefore, that the historian, surveying the past (like the statesman surveying rival powers in his own contemporary world), is apt to do less than justice to the part played by fear in politics, at any rate so far as concerns governments other than his own.

We do not always realise – and sometimes we do not like to recognise – how often a mistaken policy, an obliquity in conduct, a braggart manner, or even an act of cruelty, may be traceable to fear. What is true of individual people is likely to be still more true of great agglomerations of humanity, where further irrational factors always come into play. With nations, even more than with individuals, in fact, the symptoms of fear may be unlike fear – they may even be the result of an attempt to convince us of the reverse. Apart from all this, fear may exist as a more constant and less sensational factor in life, perpetually constricting very reasonable people in their conduct in the world. It may curb their natural desire to react against injustice, or (if only by the production of wishful thinking) prevent them from recognising the crimes of their own government. It can lead to small compliances and complicities, the production of 'yes men', the hardening of inherited orthodoxies and accepted ideas. There can also be a generalised fear that is no longer conscious of being fear, and hangs about in the form of oppressive dullness or heavy cloud, as though the snail had retreated into its shell and forgotten the reason, but had not the spirit to put out its feelers any more.

The extreme case, however, is the situation that Hobbes seems to have had in mind – a situation in which men are not absolutely brutish, and do not want to be brutish, but are made brutish by their fear and suspicion of one another. Each may be wanting peace above all things, but no single one of them can be certain about the intentions of the rest. They are like two men in a room, both anxious to throw their pistols away, but in a state of deadlock because each must be sure that he does not disarm himself before the other.

In other words, fear and suspicion are not merely factors in the story, standing on a level with a lot of other factors. They give a certain quality to human life in general, condition the nature of politics, and imprint their character on diplomacy and foreign policy.

It is the realm of international affairs, however, which comes closest to the last situation that has been mentioned, the situation of Hobbesian fear. Since the war of 1914 our predicament in this respect has become worse, not better, because, till that time, a considerable region of Europe had long enjoyed the benefit of stability and traditional acceptance. Here frontiers had been comparatively settled and a country like Norway had not needed to be greatly pre-occupied with its security. Much of that region has now been thrown into the melting pot. It is doomed to suffer further dislocations if ever there is a change in the distribution of power. The demand for security, and the high consciousness that we now have of this problem of security, have increased the difficulty, and increased the operation of fear in the world. Hitler demanded security for Germany, and I am not sure that he did not show more discernment about this matter than many other people. It was impossible however, for Germany to acquire the degree of security she thought she ought to have, without herself becoming a menace to her neighbours. This universe always was unsafe, and those who demand a watertight security are a terrible danger in any period of history. I wonder if it could not be formulated as a law that no state can ever achieve the security it desires without so tipping the balance that it becomes a menace to its neighbours. The great aggressors of modern times, France, and then Germany and then Russia, began by resisting aggressors, then demanding guarantees and more guarantees until they had come almost imperceptibly to the converse position. Then the world (always rather late in the day) would wake up and find that these powers were now aggressors themselves.

One of the most terrible consequences of fear and war fever is a melodramatic kind of myth-making which has been the curse of international relations since 1914. This is the source of the blight which makes compassion wither out of the world; and its results are before our eyes. Because we thought that there could never be an aggressor so wicked as Germany under the Kaiser, we determined to fight the First World War to the point of total surrender. We thereby conjured into existence two menaces still more formidable for ourselves – the Communist on the one hand, and Nazi on the other. Some men realised, even in 1914, that all we needed to do was to hold off Germany till the Russian Bear became a more formidable threat to all of us. To judge by the writing of some leading members of the British Foreign Office at the time, the intervening period would not have had to be long. In general, however, we can say that, until 1914, the world was perhaps proceeding very tolerably, save that it was beginning to get a little fevered, because, already, it had come somewhat under the dominion of fear. Those who made dark dismal prophecies about Germany could claim in the days of Hitler that their predictions had come true. But these people had their part in the producing of that nightmare situation in which their prophecies were almost bound to come true.

Fear, then, plays a greater part in life and in the course of history than we often realise, and sometimes we know that it is fear which is in operation when individuals and nations are bullying or bragging, or taking a crooked course. It may even be fear that is at work when a nation is desperately engaged in trying to convince us that it is not afraid. In spite of this (or perhaps rather because of it) one may feel a little anxious about the way in which the great powers of the earth appear to be relying on fear today. On the one hand, statesmen ought never to be too sure about the efficacy of fear in the last resort. On the other hand it is always dangerous to assume that fear can be used to cast out fear. The mere dread of having to suffer the consequences of the hydrogen bomb is not going to deter governments and peoples from starting warlike action, or intensifying this, once it has begun. In the critical instance – the case of the ruthless man who knows that he is beaten – the mere fear of retaliation will not in itself prevent desperate policies, including the actual use of the bomb.

The world can hardly ever have been so apprehensive as since the days when statesmen proclaimed that by victory in war they could bring about 'freedom from fear.' Those who can boast of their stocks of hydrogen bombs are not exempt from this fear, which numbs people and makes them think that they must take their fate passively, that their opinions and resolves can make no difference. We must not imagine that all is well if our armaments make the enemy afraid; for it is possible that, at least in the twentieth century, it is fear more than anything else which is the cause of war. Until very recently we ourselves had not lost the realisation of the fact that mounting armaments, because they intensified fear and poisoned human relations, operated rather to provoke war than to prevent it. Under the high pressure which fear induces, any minor and peripheral issue can seem momentous enough to justify a great war.

Those who refuse to recognise squarely the dominion of fear and the play of necessity in the world (especially during times of war, revolution and unsettlement) are often the very ones who refuse to do justice to man's freedom when they are called upon for an act of will. It is for this reason that a world as intellectually advanced as ours stands mute and paralysed before a great issue; and we grind our way, content to be locked in historical processes, content just to go digging our thought deeper into whatever happens to be the accustomed rut. There comes a moment when it is a healthy thing to pull every cord tight and make an affirmation of the higher human will. When we seem caught in a relentless historical process, our machines enslaving us, and our weapons turning against us, we must certainly not expect to escape save by an unusual assertion of the human spirit. The intensified competition in armaments embodies movements which have been mounting through the centuries, and providing mankind with its chief headache for a number of decades. Those who once thought it cynical to imagine that any power save Germany could be responsible for keeping the world still in arms, and now think that only Communists could be so wicked do not realise that if Russia and China were wiped out, the world would soon be rearming again, and as likely as not, the United States would be getting the blame for it. In other words, the problem of armaments is a bigger one than is generally realised, and we cannot begin to put the initial check upon the evil – we cannot begin to insert the first wedge – unless we make a signal call upon every human feeling we possess. We wait, perhaps, for some Abraham Lincoln who will make the mightiest kind of liberating decision.

If it is possible to put a personal opinion without claiming any authority for it, or asserting that it ought to have any weight, but regarding it as one of the varied views that are thrown up in a democracy, one might suggest that what is most terrifying of all in the present situation is not to have to keep discovering the crimes of the Communists; it is something much more inconvenient to us; namely, having to recognise the services which Communism has rendered in various parts of the globe. Those services have been accompanied by tyranny and oppression; but, again, it is terrifying to have to remember that this was once the chief objection to revolutionary democracy. It is not even clear that Communism, though it can be so oppressive today, does not possess colossal potentialities for future liberty – a liberty that we must not expect to be achieved before an international detente has made it more possible to have a relaxation at home. I think that, in this modern world, which in some ways is worse than people think but in some ways is better, all systems are going to move in the direction of liberty, if only somebody will open a window so that the world can breathe a more relaxed air and we can end the dominion of fear. If, however, we are unable to achieve this, the very measures which we are taking to preserve liberty in the world are bound to lead to the loss of liberty in the regions that most prize it. They are bound – if we go on intensifying them – to make us become in fact more and more like the thing we are opposing. Even those who customarily try to guard themselves against a facile and unrealistic idealism in politics might well wonder whether – now that the hydrogen bomb has been super-added – their antidoctrinairism is not becoming too doctrinaire. When there is a question of a weapon so destructive, the risk which accompanies one kind of action has to be balanced against the risks involved in the the opposite policy, or attendant upon inaction itself. When the hazard is very great in either case, it may be useful to take account of the end for the sake of which one chooses to accept the hazard.

The hydrogen bomb will presumably always have at least a potential existence in our civilisation, since the knowledge of how to make the weapon can hardly be unlearned, except in a disaster that would follow its drastic use. If we were to resort to the most destructive kind of bomb, we could hardly claim privilege for our generation or rely on any possibility of restricting the use of the weapon to a single war. We cannot argue still again that no generation past or future could possibly have to face an enemy as wicked as our present enemy. We should have to conclude that ours is a civilisation that took the wrong turn long ago, and now, by the hydrogen bomb, had to be rolled back to its primitive stages, so that, in a second Fall of Man, the world could unload itself of knowledge too dangerous for human possession. It is not necessary to take a very high perspective on these matters; it is just too crazy and unseemly when a civilisation as lofty as ours (pouring the best of its inventive genius into the task) carries the pursuit of destructiveness to the point at which we are now carrying it. Let us be clear about one important fact: the destructiveness which some people are now prepared to contemplate, is not to be justified for the sake of any conceivable mundane object, any purported religious claim or supermundane purpose or any virtue that one system of organisation can possess as against another. It is very questionable whether when it comes to the point, any responsible leader of a nation will ever use the hydrogen bomb in actual warfare, however much he may have determined in advance to do so. The weapon is dangerous to the world because it is a weapon only for men like the falling Hitler – desperate men making their last retreat. The real danger will come from the war leader who will stick at nothing because he knows that he is defeated in any case. He may be reckless even of his own nation, determined to postpone his own destruction for a week, or to carry the rest of the world down with him. As in the case of Germany when Hitler was falling, war may be protracted by the will of a handful of wicked and desperate men. On these terms we are going to be more afraid of defeating our enemy than of suffering ordinary military defeat ourselves.

It is not clear that there is much point in having the equality (or even the superiority) in terroristic weapons if, as is sometimes asserted, the enemy has the ruthlessness and the organisation to carry on a war with less regard for the sufferings of his people than is possible in the democracies. If Communism is a monstrous sadistic system, the gentle and the urbane will not easily outdo it in the use of terroristic device. By a reversal of all previous ideas on the subject of armaments, however, some people have imagined that the hydrogen bomb is the climax of blessing, the magical ' deterrent ' which will paralyse the guns and neutralise the numbers of the potential enemy. Such reasoning is precarious; and we ought to be very careful before we accept the view that ten years ago it was only the atomic bomb which deterred the Russians from a major war. A country in the position that Russia held after 1945 tends to seek to make use of its interim advantage up to any point short of a renewal of general war. It seeks to step in wherever there is a power vacuum and it probes for a power vacuum even where none exists – probes until it meets an uncomfortable degree of resistance. There seems to be no reason for believing that Russia would have meditated a full-scale war even if she had to meet only pre-atomic weapons, the weapons of Hitler's war. Short of such a conflict, I wonder what power ever went further in the type of aggrandizement in question than Russia at a time when the West held the atomic bomb while the East was still without it. It is even possible that we hoaxed ourselves with the atomic bomb, which was too monstrous a weapon for peripheral regions and problems, too terrible to use in a cause that was in any way dubious, too cumbrous for dealing with a power that was ready to skirmish with any danger short of actual war. In such a case one can even conceive the possibility of the Russians realising the situation in advance, and calling our bluff while we ourselves were not yet aware that we were merely bluffing. Whether this had already happened or not, it is just this situation – with the West deceived and the Russians undeceived – that we ought to be careful to avoid at the present day. We cannot contemplate – we cannot even plausibly threaten – a nuclear war over some of the mixed and mongrel issues which are arising (and are going to arise) in sundry sections of the globe. If it is argued that we can, and that the dread of this will be effective with the Russians, then, beyond question, the Russians are in a more general sense under the dominion of fear; for in such a case they have a right also to fear a wilful and capricious use of nuclear weapons.

Some men say that the world must perish rather than that Justice should fail – as though we were not leaving sufficient injustices unremedied on our own side of the Iron Curtain. The justice of man has less mercy than the justice of God, who did not say that because of the sins of some men the whole human race should lose even the chance of bettering itself in future. Even in peacetime the hydrogen bomb has made such a deep impression as to suggest enormous evils (greater than the evils of Communism itself) if the weapon is ever used by either party in a war. The demoralising effect on the user as well as the victim might well include a hysteria beyond all measure, the dissolution of loyalty to the state, and anarchy or revolution of an unprecedented kind. Even the sense of the possible proximate use of the hydrogen bomb – short of an actual explosion – will have the effect of creating a deep separation between peoples and their governments. We may know that war is near by two signs: firstly, when people begin to say that the hydrogen bomb is not so terrible after all; and secondly, when we are told that it is better to destroy civilisation than to tolerate some piece of barbarism on the part of that nation which happens to be the potential enemy at the moment. In fact, we have reached the point at which our weapons have turned against us, because their destructiveness is so out of relation with any end that war can achieve for mankind.

There is so great a risk in having the hydrogen bomb that there can hardly be greater risk if we unplug the whole system, and if our governments refuse to have anything to do with the weapon. Even if there were, the radical difference in the quality of these risks would cancel it; for with modern weapons we could easily put civilisation back a thousand years, while the course of a single century can produce a colossal transition from despotic regimes to a system of liberty. I am giving a personal view; but I am not sure that the greatest gift that the West could bring to the world would not be the resolution neither to use the hydrogen bomb nor to manufacture it any further. Certainly the East would hardly believe us (at least for some time) if we said we were not going to resort to this weapon for any conceivable end. We should have to take the line, therefore, that our determination was not dependent on anything that other people believed. Even if the East refused to join us in the assertion, we can declare that the hydrogen bomb is an unspeakable atrocity, not to be used in any war, and not even to be the basis of any form of threat. It is a thing not to be used even if the enemy had used it first, since the situation is a new one – the right of retaliation could mean no more than the right to multiply an initial catastrophe that could not be undone. While it is still open to us in time of peace, we might ask ourselves whether there is no conceivable weapon that we will brand as an atrocity, whether there is no horror that we should regard as impermissible for the winning of a war, because so incommensurate with the limited objects that can ever be secured by war. When we talk about using the hydrogen bomb to defeat agression, we are using dangerous language. Some day, no doubt, a wiser world than ours will use the term 'aggressor' against any people which enjoys rights, powers and possessions in a country that is not its own, and exploits these against the will of the population concerned. Sometimes we seem to be using the term is respect of peoples who are merely seeking to be freed from such oppression; in this sense I have seen the Algerian rebels described as aggressors, using violence for the purpose of securing a change in the status quo. The Anglo-French action at Suez should open our eyes to the fact that a so-called 'invasion' (though it be by armies in full array) can arise from something much more complicated than a mere cruel lust for conquest. The United Nations condemned the Anglo-French enterprise; but, even so, a hydrogen bomb on London or Paris would have been an unspeakable form of punishment.

It is sometimes argued that those who refuse to resort to the hydrogen bomb may be declining to risk themselves for the liberty of others. But nobody can calculate – and perhaps only accidental circumstances would decide in a given case – whether the use of the bomb or its repudiation would carry the greater immediate risk. In any case, we cannot say that we will not receive the bomb – we can only say that we will not be responsible for the sin and the crime of delivering it. Supposing we do have to receive it, the one thing we can do is to choose the end for which we will consent to be sacrificed. We can choose the cause on behalf of which we will die if we are going to have to die. We can do this instead of being the blind victims of historical processes, which will end by making us more and more like the thing that we are opposing. However hard we have tried in the twentieth century to make allowances in advance for the unpredictable consequences of war, we have always discovered that the most terrible of these had been omitted from our calculations or only imperfectly foreseen. One of the examples of the fact is the loss of liberty in various countries in Eastern Europe and the Balkans – the very regions whose freedom was the primary issue for which we were supposed to have undertaken two world wars.

If it is wrong to tip the balance slightly in favour of humanity and faith at such a point as this, the fact is so monstrous as to imply the doom of our civilisation, whatever decision we take on the present issue. If we picture a long line of future generations we can hardly help feeling that, even if wars of some sort continue (human nature remaining very much as it is now), we would want our successors not to hate one another so much as to think it justifiable to use the hydrogen bomb. The fact that we can contemplate such an atrocity is a symptom of a terrible degeneracy in human relations – a degeneracy which the predicament itself has no doubt greatly helped to produce. But if all this is not correct, and if we do not signally repudiate the hydrogen bomb, it is still true that in the last resort some strong human affirmation of a parallel kind may be the only way of stopping the tension and deflecting the course of development to which we are now enslaved. Some other kind of affirmation might serve a similar purpose; and amongst the possibilities at our disposal there is one which to many earnest people would come no doubt as a serious test. We have talked a great deal about the crimes of Communism, and those who are chiefly concerned with militaristic propaganda would like us to think of nothing else. We do not always realise what a tremendous area of our thinking is affected by the fact that we refuse to recognise also the services which Communism has rendered in various parts of the globe. At the very beginning of all our arguments and decisions, it matters very much if we consent to say that Communism is a benevolent thing gone wrong – it is not mere unredeemed and diabolical evil. For anything I know, its chief error may even be the same as that of both Catholics and Protestants in the age of the religious wars and persecutions – an error which has been responsible for terrible massacres and atrocities in history – namely a righteousness that is too stiff-necked and a readiness to believe that one can go to any degree in the use of force on behalf of a cause that one feels to be exclusively right. In such a case it is possible that we ourselves are making even the identical error, especially in any contemplation of the use of the hydrogen bomb. When there is a terrible impasse, it is sometimes useless to go on battering against the obstruction – one must play a trick of fatality by introducing a new factor into the case. We seem unable to subdue the demon of frightfulnesss in a head-on fight. Let us take the devil by the rear, and surprise him with a dose of those gentler virtues that will be poison to him. At least when the world is in extremities, the doctrine of love becomes the ultimate measure of our conduct.

All this represents in any case the kind of way in which to assert the human will, against the machinery of relentless process, in history. It represents also the way in which one would like to see the Christian religion working softly and in silence upon the affairs of the world at large. It illustrates the way in which religious activity may get a purchase on the wheels of human destiny which otherwise now appears to be directionless.

John Braine

PEOPLE KILL PEOPLE

John Braine, the Yorkshire novelist who burst into the ranks of Britain's best-selling and most significant novelists with Room at the Top, *wrote the following article for the Campaign for Nuclear Disarmament in April 1964.*

In order to write novels it is absolutely necessary for me to forget the existence of the H-Bomb. At least, I do as far as is possible push it to the back of my mind. Most of us in what I'll call the target countries have to do this simply to preserve our sanity. I don't think that my novels are unreal because the H-Bomb isn't much in evidence in the thoughts or conversation of the characters; in any case the consciousness of the thing is there. Any novelist above the hack level is always bound to give himself away; I'm past caring whether I can be described as committed, but I'm certainly not neutral. It isn't that I wouldn't like to be; my place is in the grandstand and not in the arena. But I was born too late: the distinction between the spectator and participant no longer exists.

I find it almost impossible to write about the H-Bomb. As far as that subject is concerned I can't separate my intelligence from my emotions. It frightens me too much; I'm the sort of person who, when confronted by the question on the Civil Defence poster about the millions of survivors, asks promptly another question about the millions of dead, amongst whom may well be me. In fact, whenever I think about the H-Bomb, I can only give way to despair, which is to say that I can only stop thinking of it. The nearest I've been able to get to an explanation of its existence is that the leaders of the world aren't human at all, but another planet's fifth column. This is a stock science-fiction situation but it fits the facts uncomfortably well. The only valid argument against this is that there would be no sense in taking possession of a world which had been made into a nuclear desert; but this was settled for me at any rate, by an authoritative rumour from America about three years ago that a bomb was being devised which would kill people but leave inanimate objects untouched. One doesn't blow a ship to pieces to get rid of the rats and mice and cockroaches: one fumigates it.

I may add that I don't really believe that the people who design the Bomb and the people who are prepared to drop the bomb are human either. In fact, I am prepared to amend my theory. Our leaders may well be human; the concept of deterrence is too inept to be anything else than human. (Traditionally we are the most backward race in the universe.) It's the scientists who are emphatically not: for they know what they are doing. The members of the Manhattan Project team and of the Hiroshima and Nagasaki bomber crews cannot transfer their responsibility to Mr. Truman. They can't plead that they were simply his instruments. It's a question of semantics just as much as of ethics. Instruments aren't flesh and blood. A notice I saw in a Liverpool gunsmith's window puts it very well: guns don't kill people, people kill people.

And at this stage it's best to put all fantasy aside. The weakness of the Martian hypothesis is that it's all too attractive. Detect the Martians, dispose of them, and you have world peace. You don't, of course, any more than you do if somehow the chance of nuclear war being started by madness or accident could be entirely eliminated. *Dr. Strangelove* is a brilliant film; but we mustn't allow ourselves to forget that a nuclear war begun by a sane man will be just as horrible as a nuclear war begun by a lunatic.

But, I repeat, people kill people. When Truman twice ordered mass murder to be committed he almost certainly persuaded himself that he was acting not only as a patriot but as a humanitarian. And beyond all doubt the sheer intellectual interest of their task enabled the scientists completely to forget the purpose of the thing that they were making. (It's likely that the blacksmith who made the Iron Maiden had much the same attitude.) The British scientist who made notes whilst flying over Nagasaki couldn't possibly have reflected even for one second upon the suffering below: he was an inhabitant of the world of nuclear physics in which there is neither suffering nor compassion, nor love nor, to be entirely fair, hate.

The responsibility belongs to the bomber crews, upon, to use again the dreadfully ambiguous phrase, the Deliverers.

From every great sin other great sins ensue: to deny a man responsibility for his actions is worse than to deny him food and drink. It's as if a new kind of sumptuary law had been passed and no-one under the rank of cabinet minister or its equivalent were permitted to have a conscience.

Nothing has changed. The bombers still go through the charade of instant retaliation: it's more than a charade, because it's extremely unlikely that the bombers can reach their targets. The phrase which the charade spells out is in fact Parkinson's Law. Whoever is in charge of Bomber Command isn't going to declare it redundant; but if it isn't, Polaris is. Sooner or later, however, the

Government, whether Conservative or Labour, is bound to step in when any manifestation of Parkinson's Law becomes too expensive and absurd: it's safe to say that within two years at the longest – presuming that any of us live so long – it will officially be discovered that the manned nuclear bomber is obsolete.

This doesn't matter. What matters is that the men can always be found who are prepared to commit mass murder and who, with perfect equanimity, hand over moral responsibility to the politicians. The problem is still there no matter how the bomb is delivered: under the sea or under the ground someone has in the end actually to do the job. I only ask that they should recognise that, far from having no responsibility for the world we live in, they are the ones who made it.

For Hiroshima and Nagasaki couldn't have been bombed if no-one had been willing to drop the bomb. It wasn't Truman who flew the plane, it wasn't Truman who pressed the bomb-release button. (The man who did defended his action in words which might well have been used by Adolf Eichmann: 'I had a definite job to do. I did it. I had orders to carry out. I carried them out.') The Cuba crisis had nothing to do with Kennedy or Khrushchev: it had everything to do with the Deliverers, Russian and American and British. A crisis is only a crisis because the Deliverers can be relied upon to obey orders. Even if the theory of deterrence is carried to its logical conclusion in the Doomsday Machine, there'll be some sort of safety catch with someone's finger upon it.

If the Doomsday Machine is built, then we may take it for granted that we shall have Doomsday. There remains the problem of what is to be done with the Deliverers.

The problem isn't one of disarmament; it never was. The test ban treaty didn't take us further away from world peace; but it didn't take us any nearer. For if the order to drop the bomb had been issued even as the delegates were signing the treaty the order would have been obeyed. If all nuclear weapons could be destroyed at this very moment, it won't alter the fact that amongst us are the men who would have used them if ordered to.

I am not proposing any sort of direct action. If one knew exactly who were the Deliverers in each nuclear country, if one had free access to them, if there weren't any other Deliverers in reserve, so as to speak – but I've already exceeded my ration of fantasy. We can't hope for a sort of mass conversion, a baptism by hosepipe, and we must abandon the notion of protest being an end in itself. If it comes to that – and I say this with the utmost respect – we have to abandon the idea of making martyrs of ourselves on any occasion. The whole purpose of CND is to prevent ourselves becoming victims. Suffering – and British prisons are, so a Czech anarchist once told me, the worst in Europe – is no substitute for thinking. Indeed, it prevents us from thinking clearly, and may even in the end make us worse rather than better. If I had an enemy, if I genuinely thought of someone as being a menace to my country's security and even to peace, I'm afraid that nothing would please me more than for him to go to prison. If he virtually sent himself there, so much the better. The public's memory is short and oddly selective: it tends to register only that a man has been to prison, not the reason for his going there.

And, I repeat, suffering isn't, unless we are exceptional cases, good for the character. The revelation not so much of absolute cruelty but of absolute inhumanity, can break a man; or it can turn him savage and cold. I'm not saying that those amongst us who have been to prison for conscience's sake have been affected in either of these ways; but I am warning would-be martyrs of the dangers of prison.

In short, the time for protest is over. The time for marching is over, the time for sit-down demonstrations is over, the time for going to prison is over, the time for splinter groups, for the little craft unions of CND, is over. The time for organisation not as a political party but as a pressure group has begun. And no pressure group can function effectively unless it has a programme in its entirety. I'm well aware that a hundred times on the CND platform I have said the exact opposite, since I honestly believed the strength of CND to be its lack of a programme in the proper sense of the word. As long as we all firmly believed in the necessity for unilateral nuclear disarmament it didn't seem that the differences between us mattered. We had our public meetings, we discussed what was to be done, we discovered that we couldn't agree; and we congratulated ourselves for being so splendidly free and forthright, reaffirmed our belief in unilateral nuclear disarmament, and sent our audience home with a feeling of having been warned and admonished rather than guided.

I was wrong. It isn't for me to say who else was wrong, but it is necessary that I acknowledge my own faults and that I recognise what the real task of CND is. It doesn't end with unilateral nuclear disarmament or multilateral nuclear disarmament or even – and more fantastic things have happened – general disarmament. As long as the Deliverers exist, there can be no possibility of world peace. As long as men make a distinction between public morality and private morality there can be no world peace; Acton, as always, was right. But it isn't really a question of morality but of logic. The

Deliverer still believes, so as to speak, that the earth is flat, and he is emotionally and intellectually involved with this idea.

I don't know exactly how the job of persuasion is to be carried out. As I have indicated, direct action is no solution; whether or not it is desirable, it is certainly impracticable. I am now absolutely certain that the only way to achieve world peace is to change men's thoughts. We are not concerned with changing human nature, we are not concerned with human emotions. We can't afford to let our own emotions, however generous and righteous, take over, we can't afford anger. It's only cool reason which will save us all.

Originally I had intended to call this article *Letter from the Front,* for the obvious reason that it's written from the firing-line. But this is the sort of play-acting we have now to dispense with. We are not fighting, we are thinking. Thoroughly and painfully we must think through the issues of war and peace. No computer can help us; for a computer is merely an electronic abacus. We mustn't let ourselves forget that we live only four minutes away from death but we mustn't let ourselves be frightened into taking any short cuts. There are none. But there are also no problems for which reason has not the solution.